CHRISTMAS cottage®

While there's no place like home for the holidays, a cottage Christmas is cozier, warmer, and more magical than any other kind.

contents

easy accents
- 10   Festive Welcome
- 14   Pops of Color
- 16   Very Merry Berries
- 20   Candied Bliss

cottage holiday style
- 24   Cozy Christmas
- 28   Stripe It Up
- 32   Simple Joy
- 34   Joyful Ribbons
- 36   Wooden Warmth
- 40   Christmas Collections
- 44   Hung with Care
- 46   Subtle Simplicity
- 50   Christmas with Presence
- 56   Iridescent Splendor
- 60   Cheerful Elegance
- 62   Rustic Fantasy
- 64   Fairy-tale Setting

gifts to make memories
- 72   Recipes for Giving
- 78   Wrapped in Whimsy
- 82   Wrapped to Go
- 86   Spice of Life

festive cookbook
- 92   Rise & Shine
- 98   Christmas Buffet Style
- 100   Turkey Tradition
- 104   Tiny Appetizers
- 108   Bits of Flavor
- 110   Ornament Swap Party
- 116   By the Fireside
- 120   Seasonal Scones
- 122   Warm-the-Heart Pleasures

- 126   Recipe Index
- 128   Craft It Quickly

COVER PHOTOGRAPH BY MAC JAMIESON

hm | books

EXECUTIVE VICE PRESIDENT/CCO **Brian K. Hoffman**
VICE PRESIDENT/EDITORIAL **Cindy Smith Cooper**
ART DIRECTOR **Karissa Brown**

EDITORIAL
EDITOR-IN-CHIEF **Phyllis Hoffman DePiano**
EDITORIAL DIRECTOR **Cindy Smith Cooper**
EDITOR **Linda Baltzell Wright**
CREATIVE DIRECTOR **Mac Jamieson**
ART DIRECTOR **Tracy Wood-Franklin**
ASSISTANT EDITOR **Katie Wood**
EDITORIAL ASSISTANT **Haley Bridges**
COPY EDITOR **Lauren Helmer**
CONTRIBUTING STYLIST **Yukie McLean**
SENIOR PHOTOGRAPHERS **John O'Hagan, Marcy Black Simpson**
PHOTOGRAPHERS
Sarah Arrington, William Dickey, Stephanie Welbourne, Kamin Williams
TEST KITCHEN DIRECTOR **Janice Ritter**
EXECUTIVE CHEF **Rebecca Treadwell**
TEST KITCHEN PROFESSIONALS
**Melissa L. Brinley, Kathleen Kanen, Janet Lambert,
Aimee Bishop Lindsey, Elizabeth Nelson, Anna Theoktisto, Loren Wood**
TEST KITCHEN ASSISTANT **Anita Simpson Spain**
SENIOR DIGITAL IMAGING SPECIALIST **Delisa McDaniel**
DIGITAL IMAGING SPECIALIST **Clark Densmore**
WEB DESIGNER **Glenda Cunningham**
SPECIAL PROJECTS DIRECTOR **Brenda McClain**

DIGITAL MEDIA
DIGITAL MARKETING DIRECTOR **Jon Adamson**
MULTIMEDIA DIRECTOR **Bart Clayton**
ONLINE MARKETING MANAGER **Eric Bush**

CONSUMER MARKETING
CONSUMER MARKETING DIRECTOR **Tricia Wagner**
CONSUMER MARKETING DESIGNER **Julie Haggard**

ADMINISTRATIVE
HUMAN RESOURCES DIRECTOR **Judy Brown Lazenby**
IT DIRECTOR **Matthew Scott Holt**
PRODUCTION ASSISTANT **Rachel Collins**

hm hoffmanmedia

PRESIDENT **Phyllis Hoffman DePiano**
EXECUTIVE VICE PRESIDENT/COO **Eric W. Hoffman**
EXECUTIVE VICE PRESIDENT/CCO **Brian Hart Hoffman**
EXECUTIVE VICE PRESIDENT/CFO **G. Marc Neas**
EXECUTIVE VICE PRESIDENT/FINANCE **Michael Adams**
VICE PRESIDENT/MANUFACTURING **Greg Baugh**
VICE PRESIDENT/EDITORIAL **Cindy Smith Cooper**
VICE PRESIDENT/CONSUMER MARKETING **Silvia Rider**
VICE PRESIDENT/ADMINISTRATION **Lynn Lee Terry**

Sign up for *The Cottage Journal's* newsletter at *thecottagejournal.com*.

EDITORIAL OFFICE
1900 International Park Drive, Suite 50, Birmingham, AL 35243
Phone: 205-995-8860, 888-411-8995   Fax: 205-380-2740
Website: *thecottagejournal.com*

Copyright © 2013 by Hoffman Media
Publishers of *The Cottage Journal* magazine

All rights reserved. No part of this book may be reproduced or transmitted in any form or by any means, electronic or mechanical, including photocopying, or by any information storage and retrieval system, without permission in writing from Hoffman Media. Reviewers may quote brief passages for specific inclusion in a magazine or newspaper.

Hoffman Media
1900 International Park Drive, Suite 50
Birmingham, Alabama 35243
www.hoffmanmedia.com

ISBN #978-0-9770069-9-1

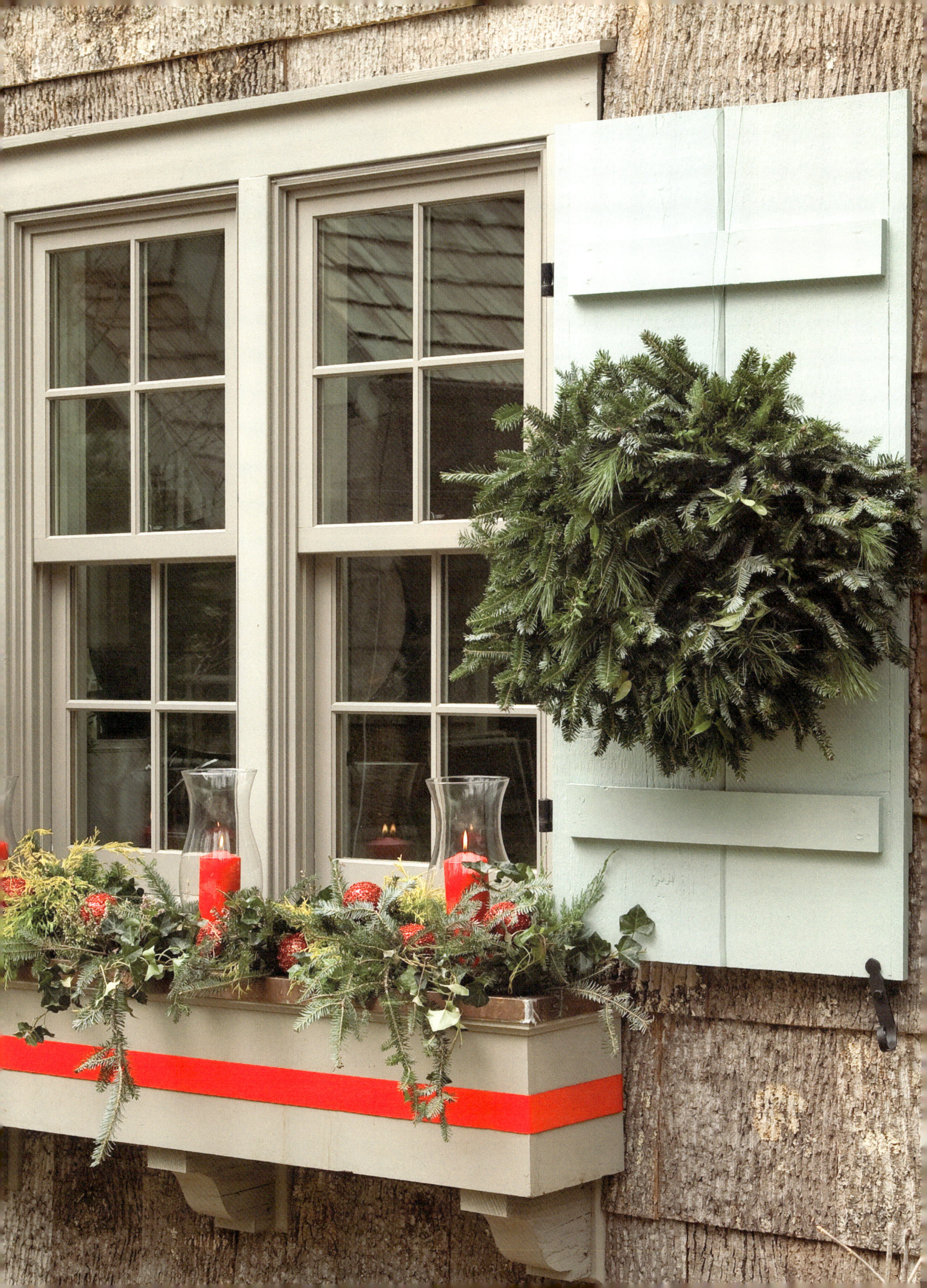

Warm Greetings

Welcome to our special holiday issue filled with ideas for a joyous, delightful Cottage Christmas.

A mixture of handcrafted and carefully selected decorations from years gone by may be your style, or you may prefer to "freshen up" your décor this year. Whatever your desire, you'll find looks to create a beautiful backdrop for seasonal entertaining and the many memories that come along with the holidays.

If you don't want to redo your entire home at once, think about adding new bows, wreaths for doors, or mantel decorations this Christmas. From a quick and natural fresh fruit and greenery look to an elegant and shimmering designer look, we're certain we have something to perfectly echo the soul of your home.

In this issue we showcase keepsake collections, as well as newer and more modern options. Some of our ideas include simple, creatively handcrafted trees like the one shown at right (photographed at the general store in the Mountaintop community of Cashiers, North Carolina). Other trees glisten with newly purchased ornaments in various sizes and colors for a bold and bright statement. Draped with ribbon and garland, they become a magical place to gather and share gifts. Your home's style and décor are a reflection of you, so make choices that bring comfort and cheer.

The simple pleasures of baking and making homemade gifts for friends and family create special heartwarming memories—after all, it's better to give than to receive! We've devoted some pages of this collector's issue to recipes and ideas to share with others.

We hope you enjoy this special issue in celebration of this glorious Christmas season. We wish for you and yours a wonderfully happy and fruitful new year ahead!

Cindy

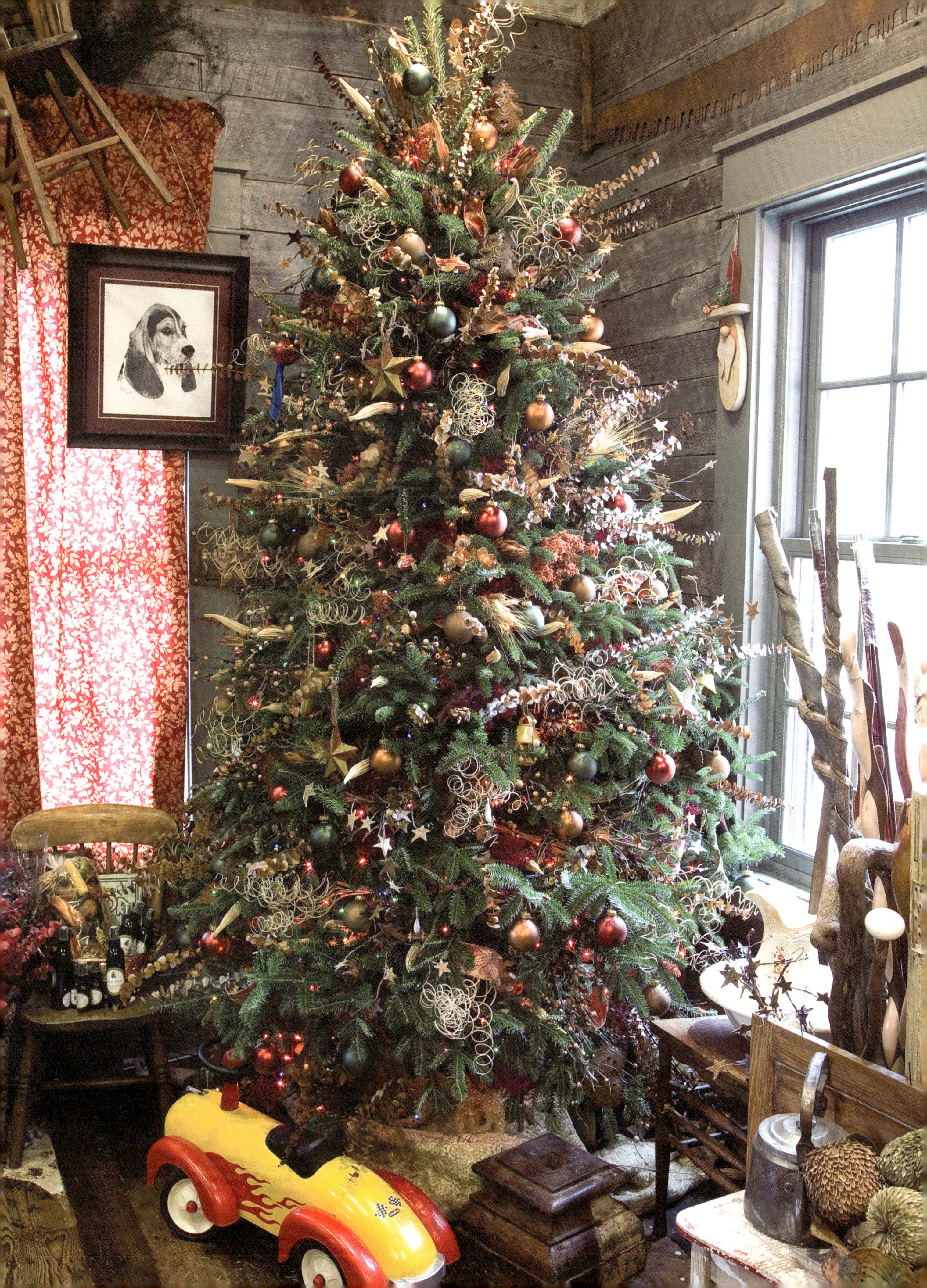

easy ACCENTS

When decorating for the holiday season, it's the little things that matter most. Sweet accents of fresh fruit, flowers, ornaments, and knickknacks reflect your personal style and the theme for your home. These are the pieces that sparkle and boast of all this season offers.

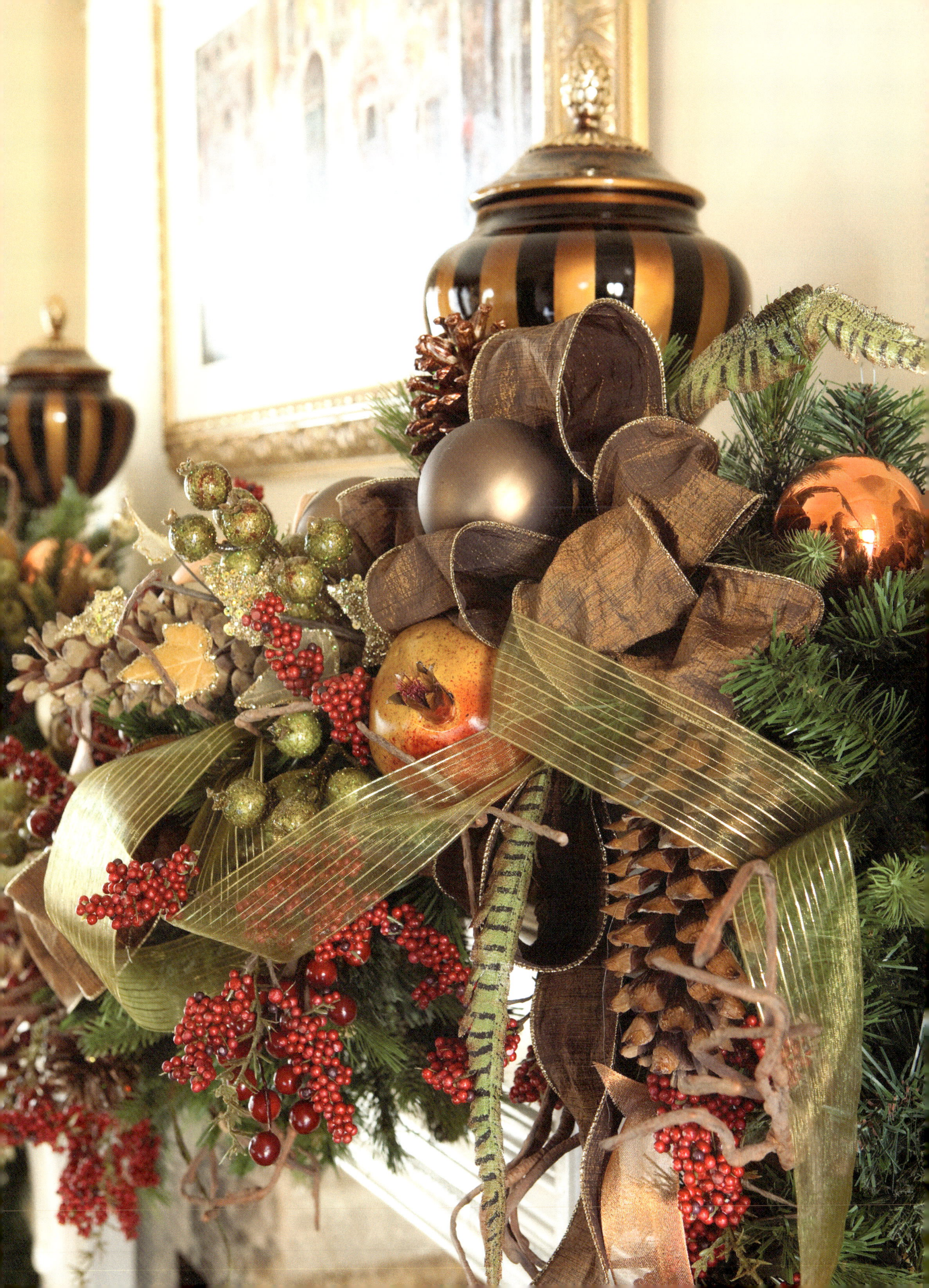

easy
ACCENTS

Festive Welcome

SERVING AS A WARM WELCOME TO YOUR HOME, WREATHS ARE A HOLIDAY STAPLE—ALWAYS ADDING THAT SPECIAL TOUCH OF MERRY AND BRIGHT.

A simple woven basket is filled with fresh foliage picked up right from the yard. It's decorated with a natural white and green ribbon and two bells that make a joyful jingle every time the door is opened.

mix it up

Don't be afraid to use vibrant colors for the holiday season. Add some life by bringing in bright greens, golds, reds, pinks, and other happy colors. Colorful ribbons also make a bold statement.

CHRISTMAS cottage | 11

✣ All you need to fashion a fabulous holiday wreath is a bit of creativity and some exciting embellishments. In no time, you'll have the perfect piece for welcoming guests during the holiday season.

{1} Create a new kind of greeting with a sweet "tweet-tweeting." A lime-tinted birdcage accented with candy stripes boasts a glittery gathering of feathers and beads. {2} A merrily metallic grapevine ring of golden pinecones and bountiful bay leaves offers guests a rich reception. {3} Add a warm welcome to a cold iron gate by hanging a tin Christmas cone overflowing with pheasant feathers, decorative globes, and tiny bright berries. {4} A charming vintage piece holds this fanciful gathering of freshly picked foliage and blush-colored berries. It brings a touch of whimsy and showcases your unique sense of style.

CHRISTMAS cottage | 13

easy ACCENTS

Pops of Color

ORNAMENTS AREN'T JUST FOR THE CHRISTMAS TREE. IN FACT, THEIR SHIMMERY, SHINY DESIGN OFTEN ADDS LIFE TO ARRANGEMENTS OF GREENERY, WREATHS, AND CENTERPIECES THROUGHOUT THE HOME.

CLOCKWISE FROM TOP LEFT: A wreath sparkles with the addition of multiple glass ornaments of differing colors and sizes. Bright red candles and glittery red ornaments bring a window box to life. Stack several intricately designed ornaments inside an old wooden box for a simple but charming effect. Using ornaments in your décor needs no rhyme or reason. Just place anywhere you want to add color and character—the possibilities are endless.

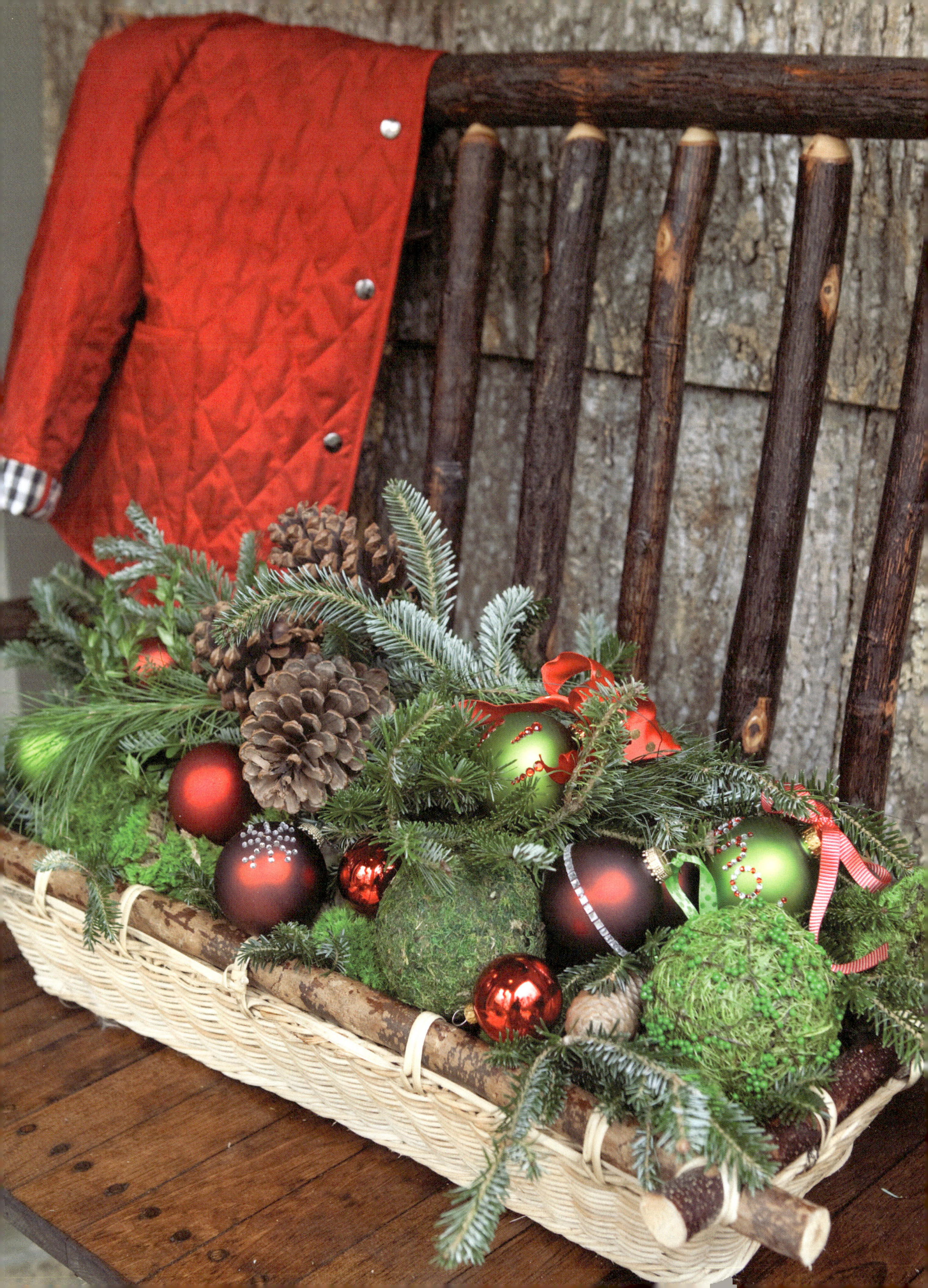

easy ACCENTS

Very Merry Berries

BRINGING THE OUTDOORS INSIDE BRINGS ALONG ENCHANTING ELEMENTS TO INSPIRE A QUIET BUT LIVE SETTING FOR YOUR COTTAGE CHRISTMAS.

Fill your newly glamorized containers with strands of beads, dried fruit, or marbles to surround the candle of your choice. Complete the design with a neatly tied ribbon or a small sugared-fruit wreath.

A full wreath of cranberries brings a simple front door to life. Streamers of red and green ribbons and a big beautiful bow add the finishing touches to this festive arrangement.

CHRISTMAS **cottage** | 17

CLOCKWISE TOP TO BOTTOM: Sprigs of holly berries and a glittery ring adorn each napkin at the table. A woodsy wreath fashioned of leaves and berries serves as a unique centerpiece when placed inside a vase. Shiny ornaments dress up the outdoorsy piece. Beautiful crystal and china are set atop the dining room table ready for entertaining. And an old St. Nick draped in leaves, pinecones, and berries holds court. OPPOSITE: Simple berry leaves brighten up the kitchen doors, and foliage that looks as though it was plucked from the woods behind the house serves as a centerpiece.

18 | CHRISTMAS cottage

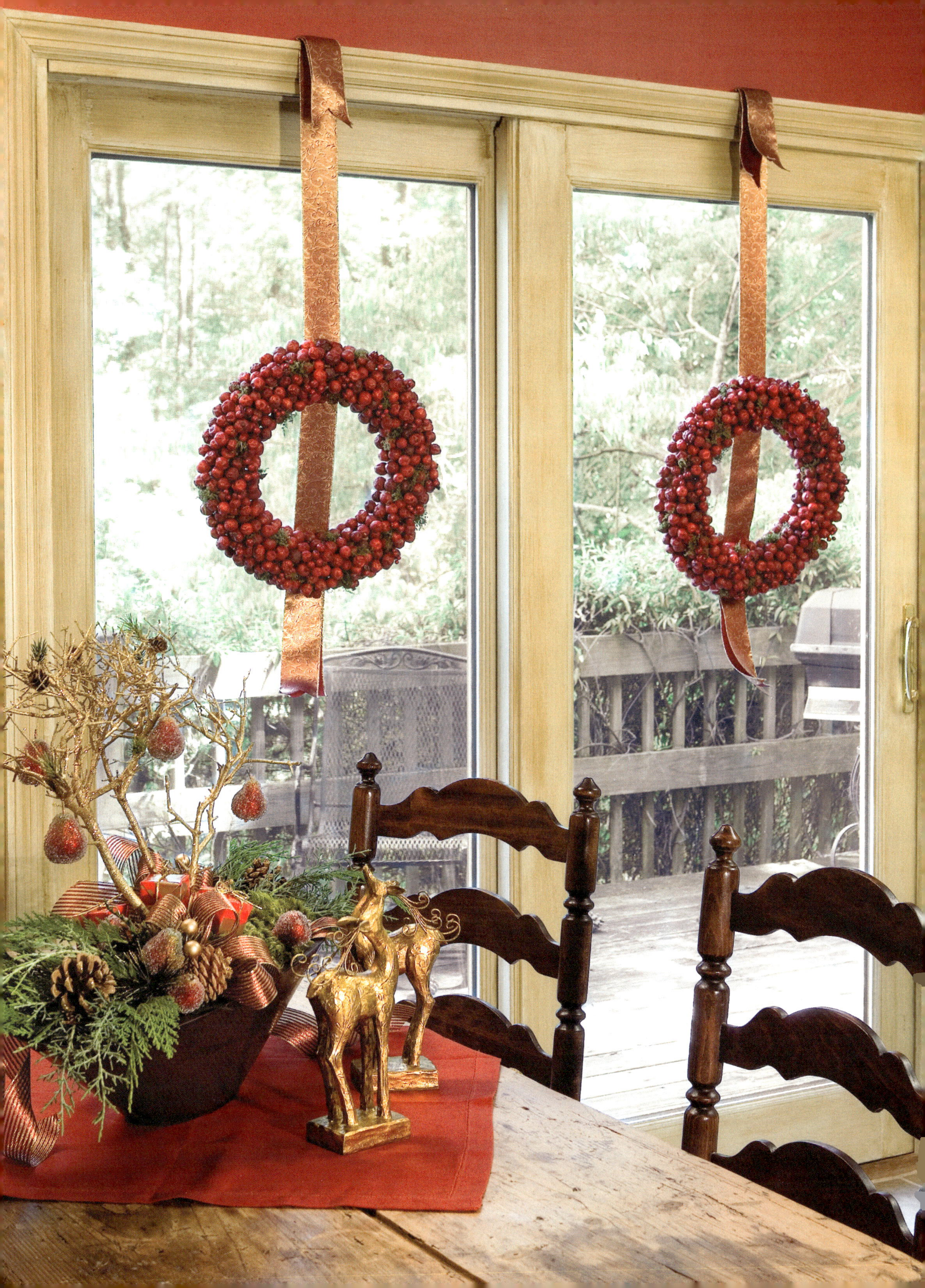

easy ACCENTS

Candied Bliss

HARD CANDIES IN THE BRIGHT, CHEERFUL COLORS OF THE SEASON MAKE SWEET ACCENTS TO YOUR HOLIDAY DECORATING. YOU JUST HAVE TO RESIST THE TEMPTATION TO NIBBLE ON YOUR CREATIONS!

ABOVE: Candy accents are delightful additions—on the Christmas tree, at the table, and poking out of stockings. With some hot glue and a little imagination, beautiful candy creations come to life. Be sure to use hard candies that have "staying power" through the season. OPPOSITE: Large Styrofoam balls are covered in peppermints and other hard candies of your choice. Simply glue on with hot glue, and hang from ribbons tied to the tree or the chandelier. Or put a stick in the bottom of the ball, and stand your beauties up in terra-cotta pots or glass jars or vases.

20 | CHRISTMAS cottage

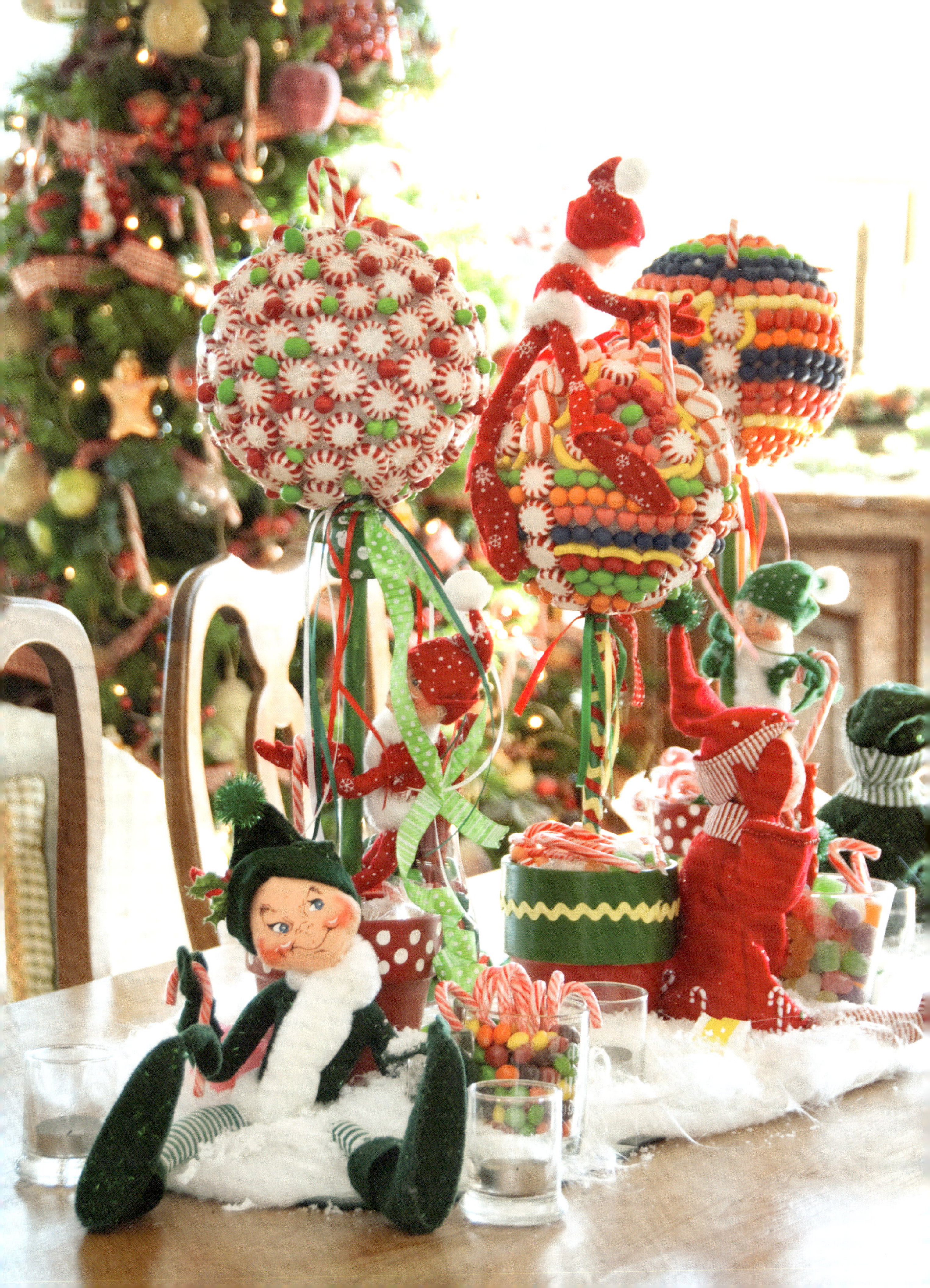

cottage
HOLIDAY STYLE

There's something cozy and comfortable about a cottage Christmas. The house is filled with special things that whisper of the season, and the accents are as warm as the crackling fire. It's simple and elegant—never extravagant. It's a place created for family to gather and enjoy the blessings of this most special time.

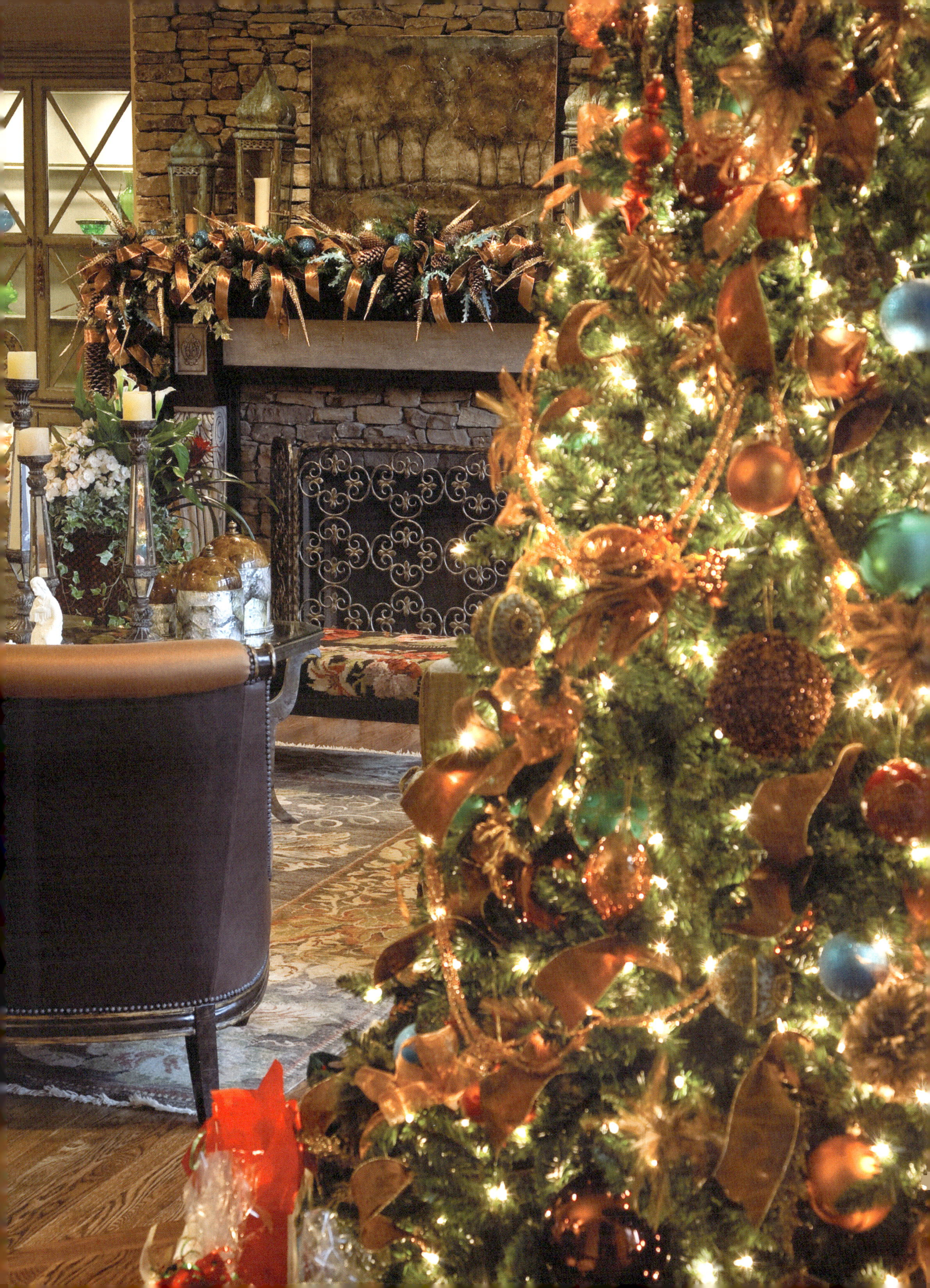

cottage
HOLIDAY STYLE

Cozy Christmas

THE TABLE IS SET AND READY FOR CHRISTMAS DAY, AND THE STOCKINGS ARE HUNG FROM THE MANTEL. THE COTTAGE HAS BEEN MADE EXTRA COZY FOR FAMILY AND FRIENDS TO GATHER TOGETHER.

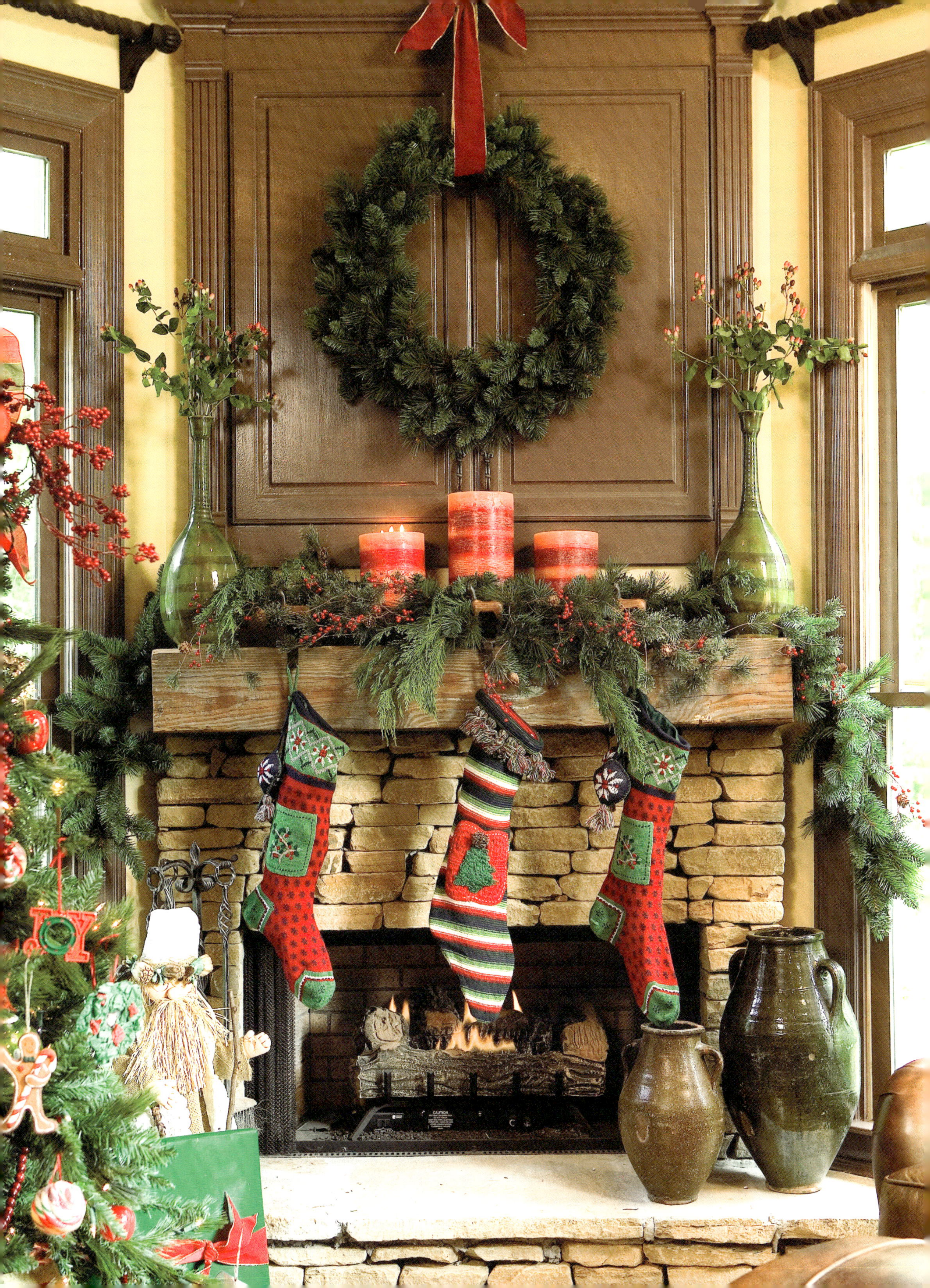

❈ Filled with nostalgia for years gone by and anticipation for those yet to come, Christmas invites family home to take pleasure in the traditions we've come to know and love. Seasonal shades of red, green, and gold join touches of orange and amber to create an ambiance so rich and warm that the morning chill simply melts away.

OPPOSITE: Dangling at the ends of ribbon streamers, pears suspended from the chandelier easily transition from Thanksgiving to Christmas. To create even more impact, consider adding traditional fruits in varying lengths to the light's base.

26 | CHRISTMAS cottage

CHRISTMAS cottage | 27

cottage
HOLIDAY STYLE

Stripe It Up

A LITTLE SWASH OF RED AND WHITE ON THE CHAIRS, WINDOWS—AND PRESENTS, TOO—CAN GET YOU INTO THE HOLIDAY MOOD IN A FLASH!

A holiday kitchen and dining room setting uses whimsical touches to welcome guests. Dining room chairs wear cloth scarves with ribbon and faux candy ties, while the kitchen chairs are simply wrapped in striped ribbons. Dots, elves, and make-believe candies adorn chandeliers, windows, and packages. A shelf in the beverage service area of the kitchen is emptied to display a Christmas scene complete with a miniature tree and snowmen. A tray of snowman glasses and peppermint-swirled mugs awaits the pourable holiday cheer!

CHRISTMAS cottage | 29

The chair embellishments say "Come and sit down with us," while candy trees and packages invite curiosity—and an appetite! At the kids' table, a red-and-white polka-dot runner sits atop a white tablecloth to add contrast to the stripes.

The adult table is a little glitzier with shiny presents piled high and elegant candlesticks that match the beautiful Christmas china. Stitched-on hardware clips dangle solid red balls and candy ornaments just for fun.

CHRISTMAS cottage | 31

cottage
HOLIDAY STYLE

Simple Joy

AMID THE GLITZ AND GLITTER OF LAVISH HOLIDAY DISPLAYS, A DECIDEDLY SIMPLE STYLE OF DECORATING CELEBRATES THE WARMTH OF CHRISTMAS.

❄ Although the whirlwind of activities and extravagant displays synonymous with the season are all part of the excitement, there are times when simplicity makes a welcome appearance. Gather the family around the table for a Christmas morning brunch that relies on subtle Yuletide symbols to make the setting sing.

Welcome everyone with ribbon-wrapped chairs sporting holly ornaments caught up in bows, then delight them with a beautiful centerpiece of white roses, baby's breath, and hypericum berries surrounding pillar candles. Use coordinating linens, berry-bedecked dinnerware, and festive glasses for a cheerful touch, then hang an eye-catching wreath at the window to preside over this simple but heart-warmingly perfect occasion.

ABOVE, TOP TO BOTTOM: Little details tie this look together. The sprinkling of ornaments around the table is echoed in the appliquéd napkins that are wrapped in wreath rings, a nod to the window display. The Holiday Gatherings pattern from Lenox is a perfect choice for this setting. Add tiny beribboned "shopping bags" for adorable place cards, then a table runner that matches the napkins to complete this pretty Yuletide presentation.

CHRISTMAS cottage | 33

cottage
HOLIDAY STYLE

Joyful Ribbons

RIBBONS ARE AN EASY AND COST-EFFECTIVE WAY TO ADD COLOR AND LIFE TO YOUR HOLIDAY DÉCOR. THEY CAN BE FANCY AND FRILLY OR CUTESY AND CASUAL, BUT THEY ALWAYS BRING JOY TO THE HOME.

There are many ways to incorporate ribbon into holiday decorating, and one special way is by fashioning a wreath. A ribbon wreath is cheerful and can be used year after year. It's easy to put together and fun to choose different ribbons to accent the room. Another delightful way to use ribbon is to take an old tablecloth and cut holes along the edges to stream long ribbons through. It's quick and adds festive pops of color to the room. Shiny glass ornaments hang from sheer ribbons tied to the chandelier over the dining room table.

CHRISTMAS cottage | 35

cottage
HOLIDAY STYLE

Wooden Warmth

RED AND GREEN MAKE THIS KITCHEN AND FAMILY AREA SING FOR THE HOLIDAYS. NATURAL CABINETRY AND WINDOWS ARE A LOVELY BACKDROP FOR LETTING DECORATIONS SHINE!

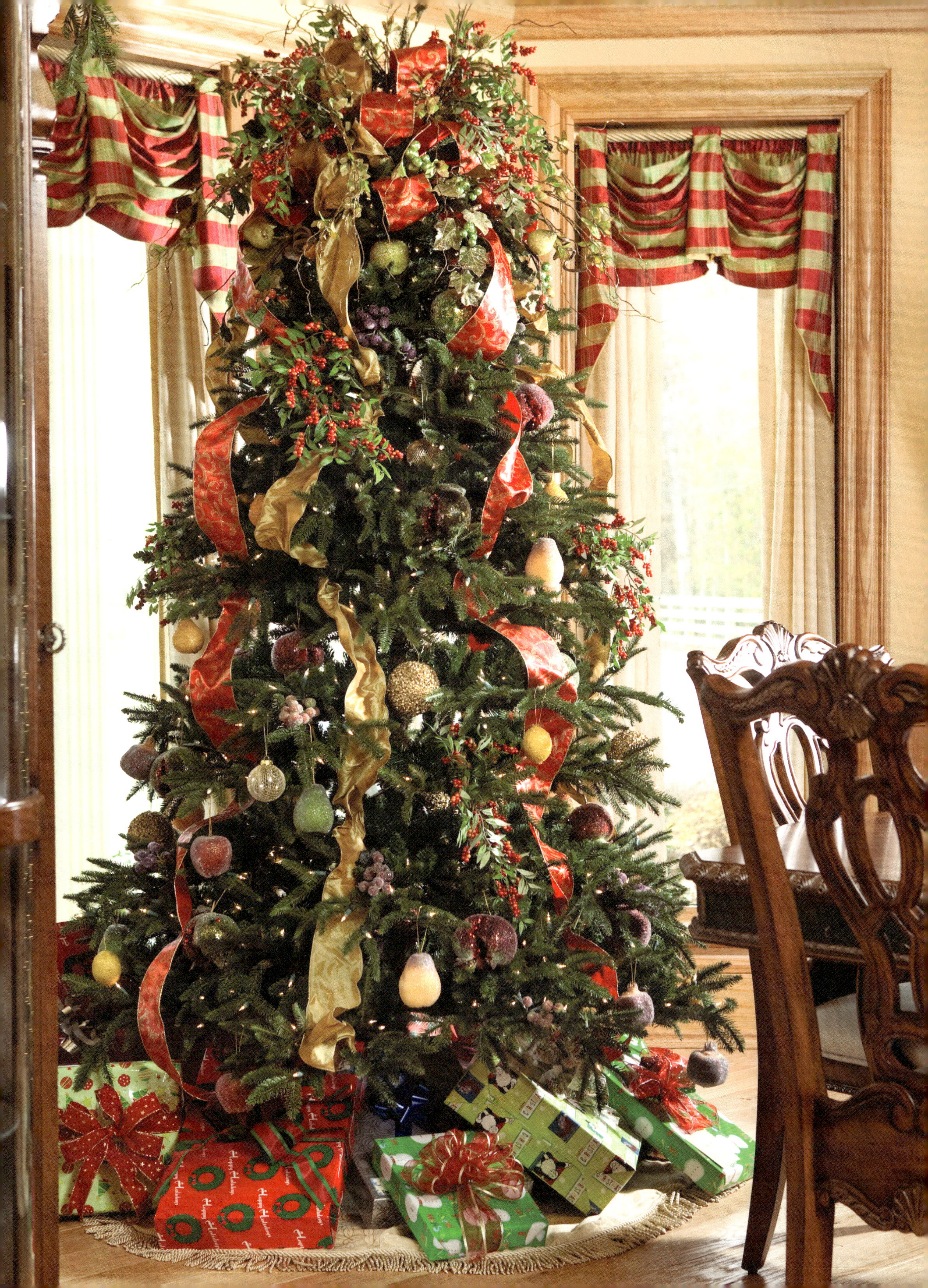

38 | CHRISTMAS cottage

❦ A comfortable cottage full of exposed beams, beautiful crown molding, and rustic brickwork doesn't require glitz or glam for the holidays. This home is clutter-free, with decorations adding touches of festive cheer in just the right places.

Greenery drapes gently across the kitchen cabinets and the china cabinet, and knickknacks are stowed away behind glass cabinets. The table displays a beautiful centerpiece, and big and small Christmas trees softly twinkle in the main living areas for all to enjoy.

CHRISTMAS cottage | 39

cottage HOLIDAY STYLE

Christmas Collections

PASSED DOWN FROM GENERATIONS OR STARTED SIMPLY AS A SPECIAL HOBBY, CHRISTMAS COLLECTIONS ARE A JOY TO PULL FROM THE ATTIC. IT'S ALMOST AS IF THEY COME ALIVE IN AN ENCHANTING WAY YEAR AFTER YEAR.

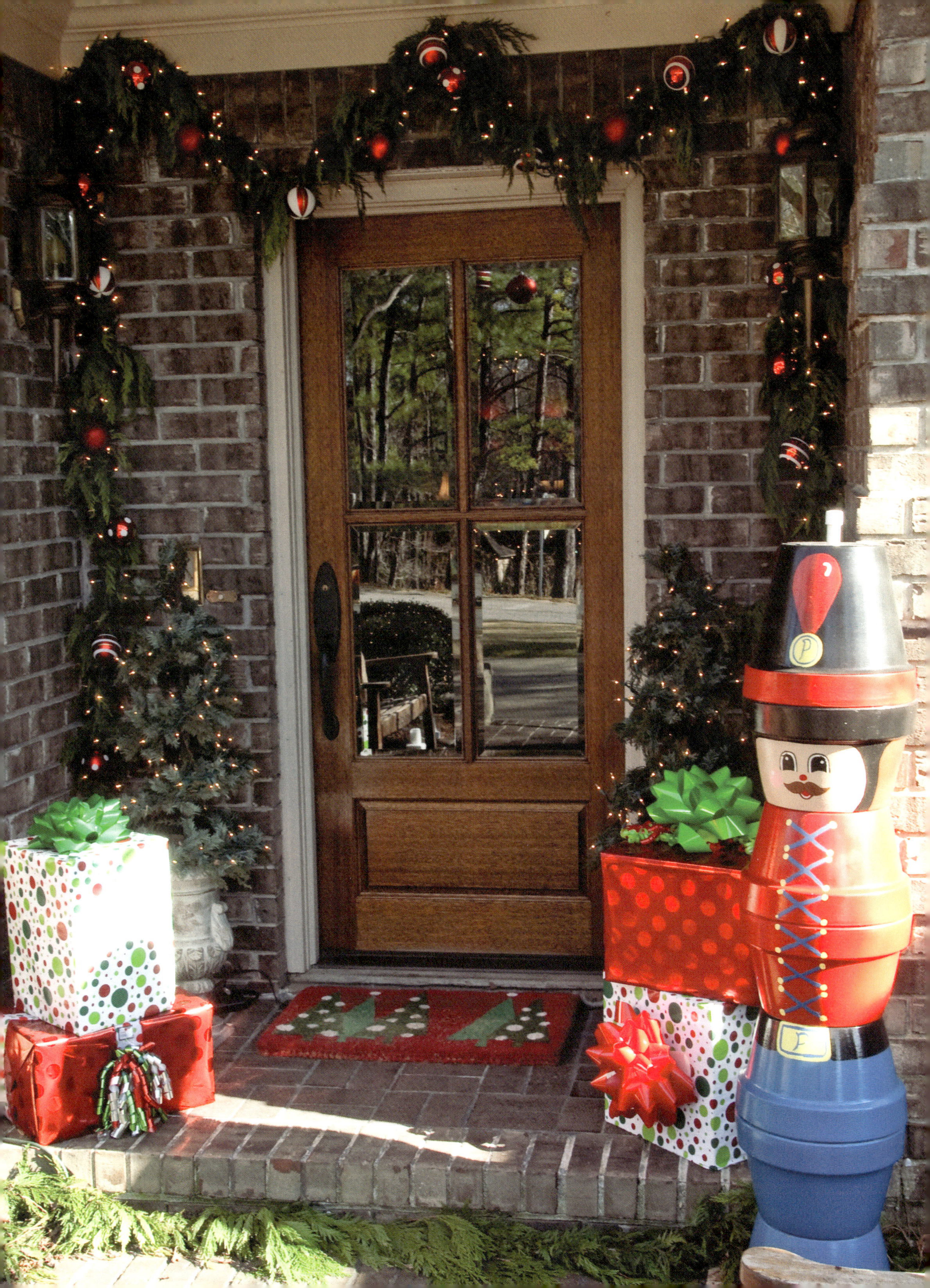

WHETHER *nutcrackers,* GLASS ORNAMENTS, HOLIDAY CHINA, OR *special gifts from loved ones,* COLLECTIONS MAKE A BEAUTIFUL ADDITION *to your home*.

❆ Nutcrackers are one of the most popular collections at Christmas. It's no wonder, because for many families, these beautiful handcrafted pieces are traditional mementos. The intricate detail that goes into carving the figures makes each one special.

CHRISTMAS cottage | 43

cottage
HOLIDAY STYLE

Hung with Care

HOME IS THE BEST PLACE TO BE FOR THE HOLIDAYS—WHERE MOM MAKES FAVORITE MEALS TO ENJOY, A CHRISTMAS TREE FULL OF FAMILIAR ORNAMENTS STANDS IN THE FAMILY ROOM, AND DAD READS *THE NIGHT BEFORE CHRISTMAS* ON CHRISTMAS EVE.

Personalized stockings hung by the chimney make every family member feel they have a special place at home for the holidays, whether they live there or have moved across the country. Some families lovingly pull out the same decorations every year, with only a few new baubles here and there—a meaningful reflection of all of the happy holiday seasons spent together.

44 | CHRISTMAS cottage

CHRISTMAS cottage | 45

cottage
HOLIDAY STYLE

Subtle Simplicity

OFTEN, THE SIMPLER THE BETTER, AND FOR HOLIDAY ENTERTAINING, UNDERSTATED WHISPERS OF THE SEASON CAN MAKE A LASTING IMPRESSION.

❈ The owners enjoy entertaining during the holidays, so they keep their rooms simple and clutter-free to host many guests. A plain wreath of red berries introduces the theme as guests enter to find a fresh fir tree with a homemade star on top and two tree forms atop the buffet in the dining room—all bare but for the single garlands winding around them. Candles bring ambience and a sweet scent to the room, but the guests are the main attraction in this cottage setting.

CHRISTMAS cottage | 47

✣ Just as the front porch reflects the laid-back attitude of the homeowners, so does the classic approach to celebrating the holidays. Fresh greenery and foliage that look as though they were scooped from the yard are the fanciest decoration you'll find. China and crystal are subtly placed throughout the home—not touting a grand occasion but rather a comfortable and cozy kind of Christmas.

candlelit glow

When decorating for the holiday season—whether your style is elegant and sophisticated or simple and classic—keep in mind the importance of candlelight. There's something magical about lighting a room with the soft glow of candles on a cold winter's night.

48 | CHRISTMAS cottage

CHRISTMAS cottage | 49

cottage
HOLIDAY STYLE

Christmas with Presence

AN ELEGANT AND REFINED APPROACH TO HOLIDAY DÉCOR GIVES A COTTAGE'S OPEN FLOOR PLAN A UNIFIED, UNCLUTTERED, BUT FESTIVE LOOK. THE SPACE IS LEFT WIDE OPEN AND FREE TO ENTERTAIN DURING THE HOLIDAY SEASON.

wrapped in white
Light and bright makes small cottage spaces feel larger, as does increasing the vertical space by raising the ceiling to the roofline. The tall, narrow white holiday tree brightens the room while taking up little space.

CHRISTMAS cottage | 51

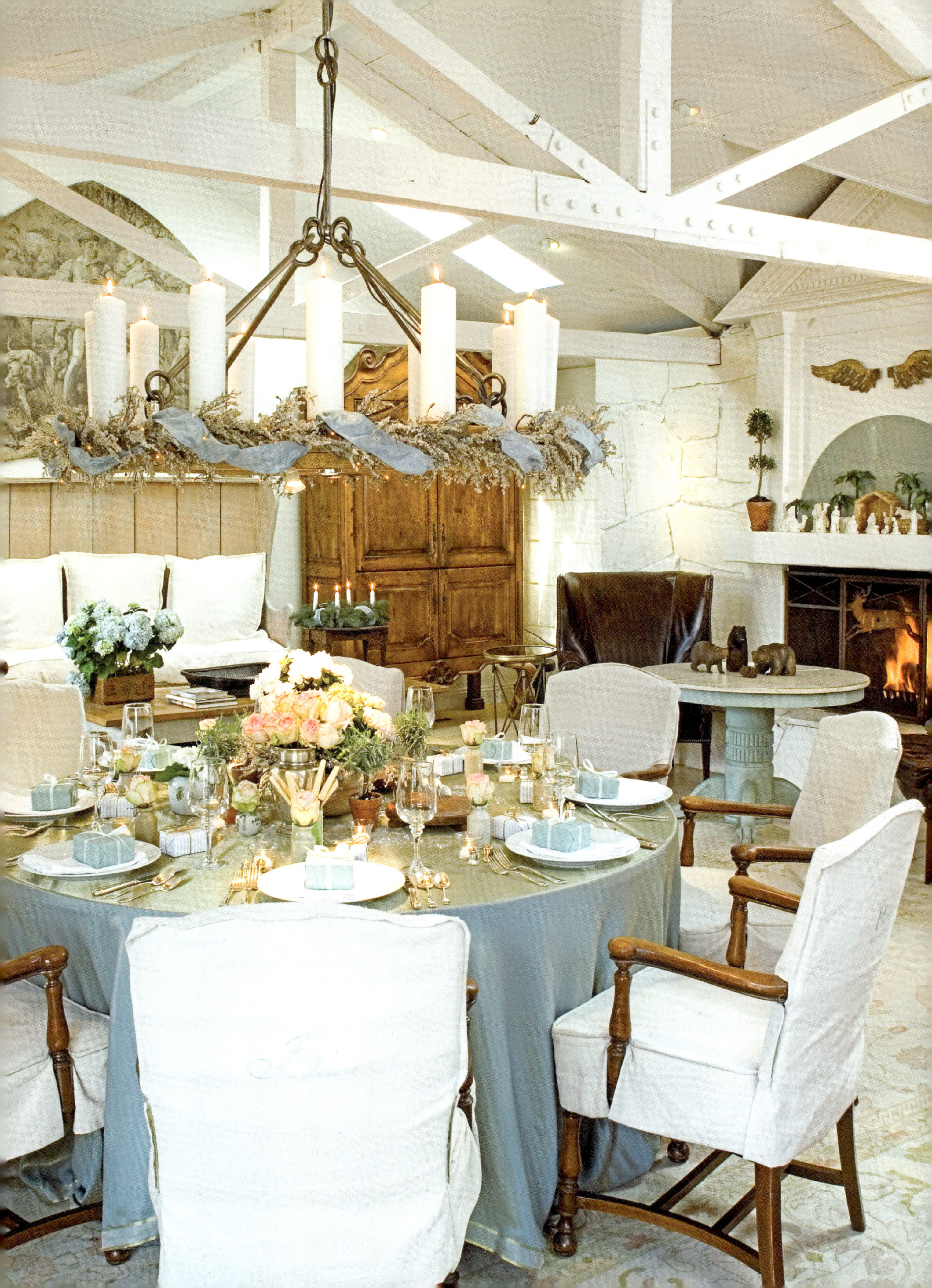

❊ This home's open floor plan wraps around a central core. The colors are a soft white that repeats in the walls, matching slipcovers, and a light wash on the fir-plank floors. A warm robin's-egg blue serves as the primary accent color in pillows and a painted pedestal table.

keep it simple

An open floor plan is a design challenge that extends to trimming the home for the holidays. The same design solutions that work for the interior apply to holiday decorating. The key is simplifying through a consistent color palette, clean lines, and attention to scale.

The color theme of soft white and robin's-egg blue carries through with the use of paint, slipcovers, hand-knitted pillow covers, a hand-sewn tablecloth, and paper book covers—all things a craft-skilled home decorator can make.

❄ The holiday décor follows suit. The white-flocked tree features ornaments with the repeated blue hue. The same color is in all the gift-wrap, including the favors on the table, and the tablecloth again echoes the same blue. For variation, the hydrangeas and roses add a pastel color that doesn't compete with the overall theme. The result is an effect that decks the halls in serene, sweet color.

mix it up
Pastel flowers are a soft look with this home's color palette.

CHRISTMAS cottage | 55

cottage
HOLIDAY STYLE

Iridescent Splendor

LADEN WITH PINECONES AND AMBER-GOLDEN RIBBON, AN OTHERWISE SUBTLE-IN-COLOR LIVING ROOM CELEBRATES WITH THE EARTHY TONES OF NATURE.

back to basics
Don't forget that some of the finest embellishments for your home can be found in the backyard or alongside a country road. Simple bowls of pine needles, pinecones, and nuts add a beautiful natural touch.

CHRISTMAS cottage | 57

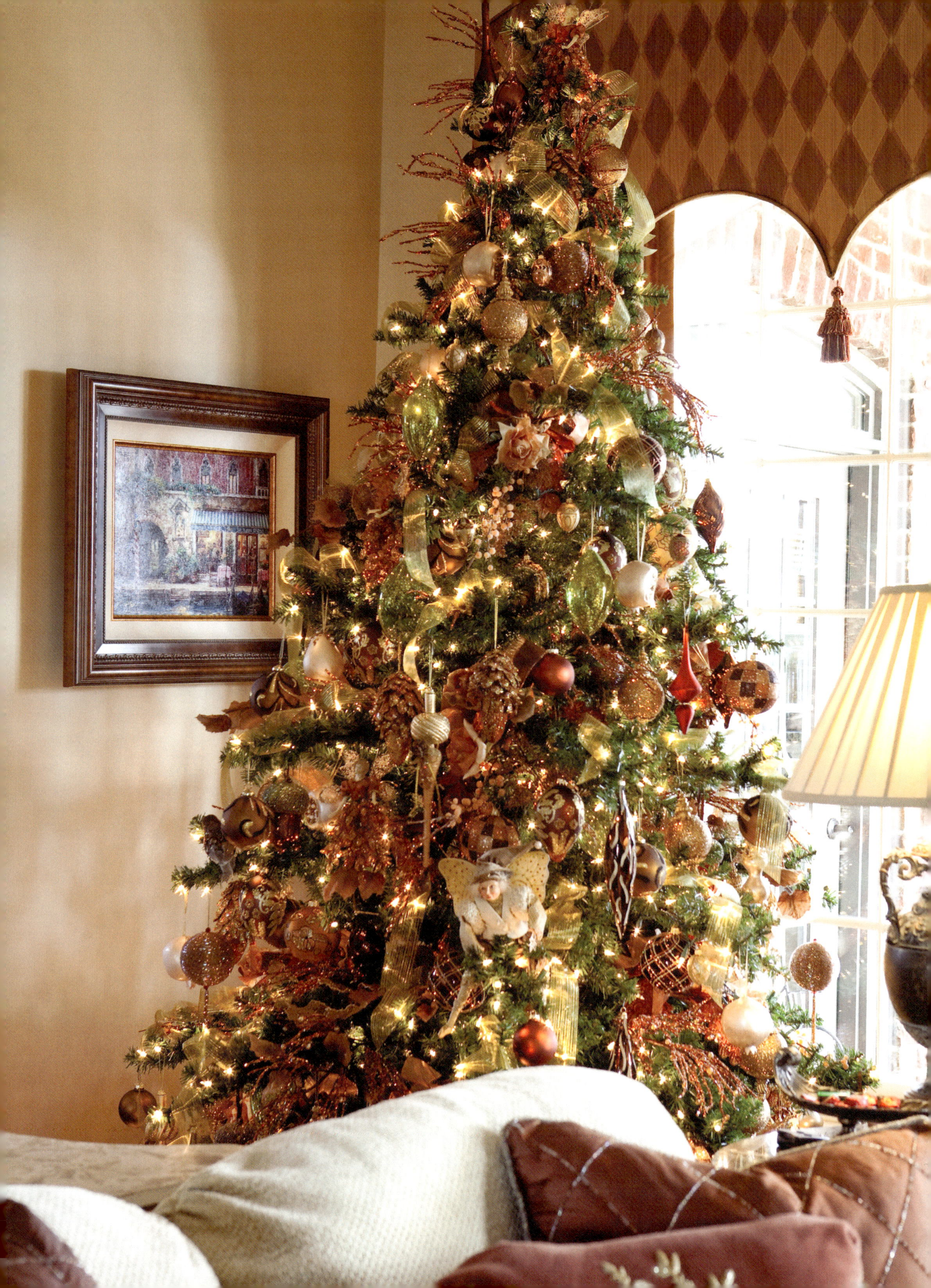

A variety of ornament shapes add interest to decorated trees, mantels, and doorways. Themes from nature, whether birds, fruit, or cones, add familiar, traditional shapes.

GOLDEN *twinkle lights* AND *ornaments* WARM THE CORNER. STOCKINGS *hang for Santa* TO *pop in* AND STUFF FULL OF SURPRISES FOR *Christmas* MORNING!

holiday welcome

Soften the doorway and the walls around the front entrance of your home to greet visitors. This doorway uses a versatile look that can last from Thanksgiving through the Christmas holidays with permanent pieces.

CHRISTMAS cottage | 59

cottage
HOLIDAY STYLE

Cheerful Elegance

BRIGHT POPS OF RED ADD EXTRA CHEER TO THIS BEAUTIFUL HOME AT CHRISTMASTIME. FROM THE OUTDOORS IN, THIS VIBRANT COLOR WELCOMES THE HOLIDAYS.

❆ This cottage exudes holiday cheer from the moment guests arrive. The breathtaking display on the front door welcomes one and all. Traditional Christmas colors are found in the greenery and red ribbons and bows of the swags. Two beautiful wreaths hang from the front-door windows to add extra color. Inside, the crimson dining room is the perfect place to entertain. The bold color of the walls means decorations can be simple. Christmas china, red napkins, and little holly sprigs atop gold chargers steal the show.

CHRISTMAS **cottage** | 61

cottage
HOLIDAY STYLE

Rustic Fantasy

THIS COTTAGE IS ABOUT MIXING ELEGANT WITH RUSTIC, AND THE CHRISTMAS DÉCOR REFLECTS THE THEME PERFECTLY.

Earthy goodness covers this home, from the warmth of the walls to the floors. Inside, the charm of the mantel and tree pairs well with the leather seating and rock walls. Blue and turquoise are woven into the array of colors, playing off the collection of glassware in the large lighted cabinet.

62 | CHRISTMAS cottage

CHRISTMAS cottage | 63

cottage
HOLIDAY STYLE

A Fairy-tale Setting
THIS QUAINT ENGLISH-TUDOR COTTAGE TUCKED UNDER STRETCHED VINES IS ALMOST HIDDEN BEHIND A MOSSY WALL. BUT INSIDE, BEAUTIFUL HOLIDAY TREASURES COME ALIVE.

4124

Because of the understated beauty of the exterior of the cottage, the owners keep holiday decorations simple but elegant. A fresh green wreath filled with seasonal fruits adorns the front door, and swags of fresh greenery frame the doorway to welcome guests.

✣ This warm home exudes classic charm. Nothing is overdone, yet every nook and cranny tell of the Christmas season. Fresh greenery and natural fruits and berries are used throughout, with each space boasting its own special touch of luxurious ribbon, colorful tassels, warm candles, or quaint Christmas stockings.

less is more

Fresh fruits, berries, and greenery not only give the space color, but fill it with a sweet aroma. These are more cost-effective than expensive ornaments and just as pleasing to the eye. White candles along the mantel offer the same twinkling glow as electric Christmas lights.

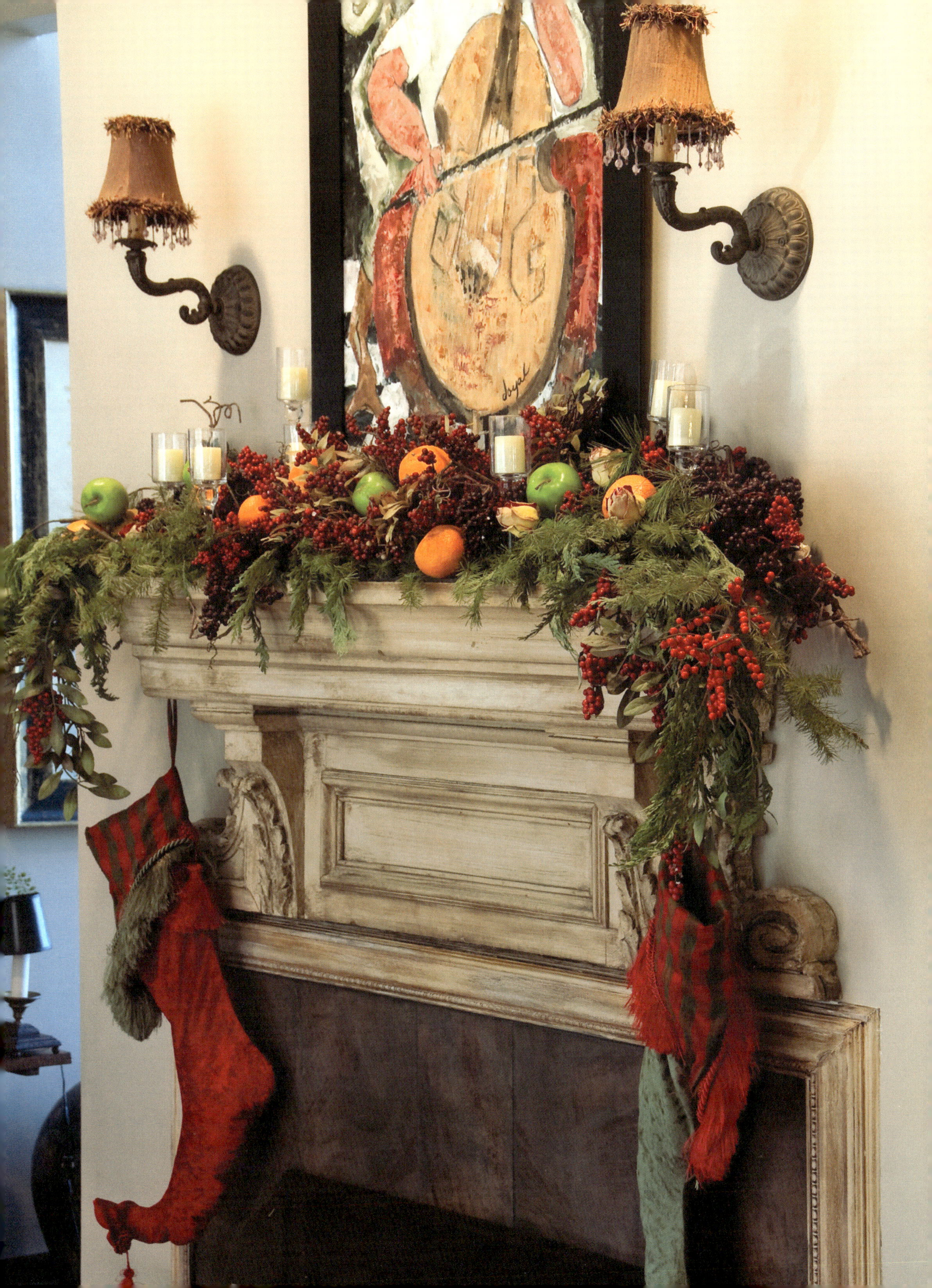

set for a king

Whether you host a holiday party or your family's Christmas dinner, the dining room must be made ready for a celebration. A lion statue peacefully rests among elegant pieces such as fine silver goblets and beautiful crystal. Fresh fruit, flowers, and greenery grace the dining room, as well as serve as a backdrop for the lion centerpiece. Silver planters line the table, and lovely Christmas china sits atop chargers and alongside glassware both accented with silver, awaiting the Christmas feast. Felt stitched place cards at each setting offer a special touch to show guests you anticipate their visit. Leave an ornament or other special item to take home from the evening, then spend time making the gathering memorable for all.

CHRISTMAS cottage | 69

gifts to
MAKE MEMORIES

Although the season isn't just for gift giving, that is a big part of the holidays. Presents leave a lasting impression when given a great deal of thought and fashioned by hand out of love. Don't think of the best things money can buy, but rather the most thoughtful things you can make.

Happy Holidays!
pretty packages
SENDING A PACKAGE OF
It's the most
WONDERFUL
time of the year

gifts to
MAKE MEMORIES

Recipes for Giving

NESTLE INTO YOUR KITCHEN, AND CREATE SOME HEARTFELT GIFTS THAT ARE SURE TO BRING A SMILE—SPICED, DECORATED, AND ALL DRESSED UP FOR A BIG HOLIDAY GATHERING OR AS A CENTERPIECE FOR CONVERSATION.

CINNAMON-SPICED CRABAPPLES

Prep Time: 25 minutes | Cook Time: 18 minutes | Processing Time: 20 minutes | Makes four to five (1-pint/½-liter) jars of crabapples

This recipe will be ideal for the cook with a crabapple tree in the yard or in a friend's yard! However, during the fall months, you'll also often see crabapples for sale at farmers' markets. These small, adorable, blushed-red apples are too hard and tart to eat out of hand, but they make incredible jams and jellies. My favorite way to preserve them is to pack them into jars whole and then fill the jar with a spice-infused, sweet pickling liquid. Once processed, these rosy orbs are suspended in a transparent, pink-tinged liquid—delectably cute and wonderful for gift giving. They make a terrific accompaniment to roast pork and poultry.

—Adapted from *Gifts Cooks Love: Recipes for Giving* by Sur La Table and Diane Morgan/Andrews McMeel Publishing. Photography by Sara Remington.

INGREDIENTS
1 (3-inch-long) cinnamon stick
3 whole star anise
1 tablespoon whole cloves
2 teaspoons black peppercorns
4½ cups granulated sugar
3 cups water
2½ cups cider vinegar
2 pounds (about 8 cups) crabapples

IMPLEMENTS
Four or Five (1-Pint/½-Liter) Glass Canning Jars, Water Bath Canner, Measuring Cups and Spoons, Kitchen Shears, Cheesecloth, Kitchen Twine, 6-Quart Saucepan, Silicone Spatula, Wooden or Metal Skewer, Slotted Spoon, Wide-Mouth Funnel, Ladle, Wooden Chopstick or Skewer, Canning Jar Lifter, Sturdy Rimmed Baking Sheet

1. Wash the jars, including the lids and screw bands, in hot, soapy water. Alternatively, run the jars through the regular cycle of your dishwasher; wash the lids and screw bands by hand. Bring water to a boil in a water bath canner. Sterilize the jars and lids.

2. Place the cinnamon stick, star anise, cloves, and peppercorns on a square of cheesecloth and tie securely with kitchen twine to form a spice bag.

3. In a 6-quart saucepan, combine the sugar, water, and vinegar. Bring to a boil over high heat, stirring until the sugar is dissolved. Add the spice bag. Decrease the heat to low, cover, and simmer for 15 minutes.

4. Meanwhile, wash the crabapples and pat dry with paper towels. Using kitchen shears, snip the stem ends, leaving ½ inch intact. Using a skewer, prick each crabapple in several places. Set aside. (This allows the spiced syrup to permeate the crabapples and reduces the amount of bursting when the fruit is heated.)

5. Add the crabapples to the pot and simmer, uncovered, for 3 minutes.

6. Using a slotted spoon and wide-mouth funnel, pack the crabapples into the hot, sterilized jars, leaving a generous ½ inch headspace. Ladle the hot syrup into the jars, covering the crabapples and leaving ½ inch headspace. Remove any air bubbles by running a long wooden utensil, such as a chopstick or wooden skewer, between the jar and the syrup. Wipe the rims clean. Seal according to the manufacturer's directions. Process the jars in a boiling water bath for 20 minutes, and then turn off the heat. Wait 5 minutes, and then lift the canning rack and, using a canning jar lifter, transfer the jars to a sturdy rimmed baking sheet lined with a double thickness of paper towels and let them rest. (Use paper towels rather than a cloth kitchen towel because the liquids might weep a bit and turn the cloth pink.) Check the seals, wipe the jars, and label.

gift-giving tip
Tie each jar with raffia or ribbon and attach a gift card. To turn this into a gift basket, consider including a package of wild rice, dry-roasted nuts, and some dried fruits—all possible ingredients for a wild rice stuffing to accompany a holiday bird.

DOUBLE FUDGE BROWNIE POPS

Prep Time: 30 minutes | Bake Time: 20 minutes per batch | Makes two dozen brownie pops

❆ Is there anything more adorable than a brownie baked in a petite mold, decorated with icing and sprinkles, and secured on a lollipop stick? No way! Think of these as party favors, sweets for your colleagues at work, Christmastime stocking stuffers, or Halloween treats. The decorating fun is up to you: The white chocolate can be tinted using food coloring to match whatever holiday you are making these for—use pink for Valentine's Day, pastels for Easter, red and green for Christmas, or even orange for Halloween.

—Adapted from *Gifts Cooks Love: Recipes for Giving* by Sur La Table and Diane Morgan/Andrews McMeel Publishing. Photography by Sara Remington.

INGREDIENTS
Vegetable oil cooking spray for preparing the pans
1 cup all-purpose flour
¾ cup plus 1 tablespoon sifted unsweetened cocoa powder
1½ teaspoons baking powder
¼ teaspoon kosher or sea salt
1 cup (2 sticks) unsalted butter, melted
1 cup granulated sugar
1 cup packed light brown sugar
3 large eggs
2 teaspoons pure vanilla extract
1 cup semisweet mini chocolate chips
6 to 8 ounces white chocolate
Red, green, or other seasonal sparkling sugars
Christmas-colored nonpareils or other seasonal holiday sprinkles

IMPLEMENTS
Wilton Silicone Brownie Pop Molds (Preferably Two or Three Molds Making Eight Pops Each), Large Rimmed Baking Sheet, Measuring Cups and Spoons, Medium Bowl, Flour Sifter, Stand Mixer with Paddle Attachment or Hand Mixer, Rubber Spatula, 1½-Ounce (#30) Ice-Cream Scoop or Small Spoon, Cooling Rack, Microwave-Safe Small Bowl, Soup Spoon, Twenty-Four Lollipop/Brownie Pop Sticks

1. Position a rack in the center of the oven. Preheat the oven to 350°F. Spray the silicone molds with cooking spray to ensure the brownie pops won't stick. Set aside on a large rimmed baking sheet.

2. In a medium bowl, sift together the flour, cocoa, baking powder, and salt. Set aside.

3. In the bowl of a stand mixer fitted with the paddle attachment, beat together the butter and granulated and brown sugars on medium speed until blended, about 3 minutes. Add the eggs one at a time, beating well after each addition. Beat in the vanilla, and then stop and scrape down the sides of the bowl once with a rubber spatula.

4. With the mixer on low speed, add the sifted ingredients in 3 batches, beating after each addition until the flour disappears. Do not overmix. Using a rubber spatula, fold in the chocolate chips.

5. Using a small spoon or #30 ice-cream scoop, portion the batter into the molds, filling each cavity two-thirds full. Tap the molds on the counter to release any air bubbles. (Reserve the batter and bake the brownie pops in batches, if necessary.) Bake the brownie pops on the baking sheet until a toothpick inserted into the center comes out clean, about 20 minutes. Transfer the molds to a wire rack and let cool completely before releasing the brownie pops.

6. To decorate, set the brownie pops, flat side down, on a baking sheet lined with parchment or waxed paper.

7. Break the white chocolate into small chunks and place in a small microwave-safe bowl. Microwave on high for 2 minutes, stirring after 1 minute, until the chocolate is completely melted.

8. Using a soup spoon, drizzle the chocolate over the top of each brownie pop, allowing the chocolate to stream down the sides to form "legs." Before the chocolate sets, sprinkle the brownie pops with sparkling sugar and nonpareils. Carefully place a brownie pop stick in the center at the top, pushing until the stick is about three-quarters of the way into the brownie. If needed, add a few more sprinkles at the insertion point of the stick. Refrigerate until completely set, about 4 hours.

gift-giving tip
Cut sheets of clear cellophane to form 8 by 10-inch rectangles. Cut ribbon into 13-inch lengths. Arrange a brownie pop in the center of a cellophane sheet. Bring up the sides and cinch closed at the top of the brownie, securing the cellophane with the ribbon and tying it around the lollipop stick. Tie a bow, and attach a gift card. Refrigerate until ready to give.

BISCOTTI CHRISTMAS TREE

Prep Time: 1½ hours | Bake Time: 40 minutes | Assembly Time: 45 minutes | Makes one large biscotti tree with about four dozen cookies of varying length

Here's a spectacular dessert and centerpiece all in one! Think of giving this biscotti tree to a friend or family member who is hosting a holiday brunch, open house, or family dinner.

—Adapted from *Gifts Cooks Love: Recipes for Giving* by Sur La Table and Diane Morgan/Andrews McMeel Publishing. Photography by Sara Remington.

INGREDIENTS
4½ cups all-purpose flour, plus more for dusting
4 teaspoons baking powder
½ teaspoon baking soda
1½ teaspoons ground cinnamon
1 teaspoon ground coriander
1 teaspoon kosher or sea salt
½ teaspoon ground cloves
¾ cup (1½ sticks) unsalted butter, at room temperature
1 cup granulated sugar
4 large eggs
2 tablespoons grated orange zest
2 teaspoons pure vanilla extract
1½ cups unsalted shelled pistachios
1 cup sweetened dried cranberries

MARMALADE ICING
4 cups (1 pound) confectioners' sugar, plus more for dusting
¾ cup orange marmalade
2 tablespoons orange juice or orange-flavored liqueur, such as Cointreau

IMPLEMENTS
Three Sturdy (15 by 12-Inch) Baking Sheets, Parchment Paper, Measuring Cups and Spoons, Sifter, Large Bowl, Zester, Stand Mixer with Paddle Attachment or Hand Mixer, Rubber Spatula, Kitchen Scale (optional), Long Plastic Ruler, Cutting Board, Long Serrated Knife, Spatula, Cooling Rack, Chef's Knife, Small Microwave-Safe Bowl, Pastry Bag and ¼-Inch Plain Tip, Large Flat Platter

CHRISTMAS cottage

1. Have ready 3 sturdy 15 by 12-inch baking sheets lined with parchment paper.

2. In a large bowl, sift together the flour, baking powder, baking soda, cinnamon, coriander, salt, and cloves. Set aside.

3. In the bowl of a stand mixer fitted with the paddle attachment, cream the butter and sugar until fluffy, about 3 minutes. Add the eggs one at a time, beating well after each addition. Mix in the orange zest and vanilla.

4. With the mixer on low speed, add the sifted ingredients in 3 batches, beating after each addition until the flour disappears. Do not overmix. Using a rubber spatula, fold in the nuts and cranberries.

5. Turn the mixture out onto lightly floured work surface. The dough will be a bit sticky. Divide the dough into 3 equal portions. (It would be ideal if you had a scale to weigh the portions. Each portion weighs 18 ounces.) With lightly floured hands, and working with one portion at a time, place the dough in the center of the parchment-lined pan. Pat each piece into an evenly thick flat-topped triangle that measures 9 inches across the base, 2 inches across the top, and 12 inches on the sides. Use a long plastic ruler to measure the sides and form clean, straight edges by pressing the ruler alongside the dough. Repeat with the remaining portions of dough. As you finish forming the triangles, place them in the refrigerator to chill for 30 minutes.

6. While the dough is resting, position one rack in the center of the oven and another rack in the lower third of the oven. Preheat the oven to 350°F. (If you happen to have two ovens or a large oven with 3 oven racks, you can bake all the biscotti at once. Otherwise, you'll need to bake the biscotti in batches.)

7. Bake the biscotti until just beginning to turn light brown at the edges, 15 to 20 minutes. Switch the pans between the racks at the midpoint of baking so that they bake evenly. Remove from the oven and cool for 5 minutes.

8. Working with one partially baked biscotti triangle at a time, carefully transfer the parchment sheet to a large cutting board. Using a long serrated knife and a ruler, begin at the base of the triangle and position the ruler parallel to the base. Using a sawing motion, precisely measure and cut the triangle into $5/8$-inch-wide slices, working your way up to the top. Repeat to cut the remaining baked triangles.

9. Place the slices on their sides on the unlined baking sheets. Bake until dried out and lightly golden, about 10 minutes. Turn each slice over and bake until lightly golden, about 10 minutes longer. Transfer to wire racks to cool completely. (The biscotti can be made 1 to 2 days in advance. Store in a covered container at room temperature.)

10. To assemble the biscotti tree, first make the marmalade icing. Sift the confectioners' sugar into the bowl of a stand mixer fitted with the paddle attachment or into a large bowl and use a hand mixer. Pick out and finely mince the pieces of orange peel from the marmalade. Add the minced peel back into the marmalade and then warm it in a microwave to liquefy it, about 30 seconds. Add the marmalade and orange juice to the sifted sugar and beat for 5 minutes. The icing will be silky and glistening, and all the sugar will be absorbed. Transfer to a pastry bag fitted with a $1/4$-inch plain tip. Set aside.

11. Have ready a large flat platter. Select the 3 longest cookies. Pipe the icing on one of the cut sides of each cookie. Lay, icing side down, on the platter with the tips touching to form a large triangle. Pipe a long thick line of icing along the length of each cookie. Select the next 3 longest cookies, and create a Star of David by arranging them in a triangle shape, with tips touching, on top of the base triangle. Pipe a long thick line of icing along the length of each cookie. Continue to build the tree by repeating this process of layering the cookies and icing each layer, selecting the next longest cookies for each layer, finishing with the small 2-inch cookies for the top. Use extra icing to drip "icicles" at the edges or along the sides. Dust the tree with confectioners' sugar "snow." Decorate the platter with holly sprigs and faux red berry clusters, if desired.

Encourage guests to sample a cookie by gently lifting a cookie from the top of the tree. The tree can be assembled and stored uncovered, in a cool, dry spot for up to 3 days.

gifts to
MAKE MEMORIES

Wrapped in Whimsy
BEAUTIFUL PRESENTATION ON THE OUTSIDE SETS THE TONE FOR THE THOUGHTFUL GIFT INSIDE.

Felix Fu's charming interpretations pair perfectly with holiday greetings in the form of baker's labels, gift tags, holiday cards, and return address labels. OPPOSITE: Recycled papers and thin chipboard pair with a stamped tree motif for a cute gift tag. Tie on with beautiful satin ribbon or cord to complement your package tops. Scalloped gift tags can be hand snipped or purchased from your favorite craft supply store.

80 | CHRISTMAS cottage

The size of a Felix Doolittle illustration and the amount of intricate detail therein create an interesting juxtaposition. In motifs such as mistletoe, holly berries, and piles of presents, Felix Fu's artwork makes every item it graces a special delivery. LEFT: Send tidings of joy to friends and family with these stunning cards by Anna Griffin. Each is embellished with tinsel and ribbon on exquisite patterns inspired by antiques and fine textiles.

CHRISTMAS cottage | 81

gifts to
MAKE MEMORIES

Wrapped to Go

ALTHOUGH THE CHRISTMAS SEASON ISN'T JUST ABOUT GIVING GIFTS, FRIENDS AND FAMILIES INEVITABLY LOOK FORWARD TO SURPRISING ONE ANOTHER WITH WELL-THOUGHT-OUT GOODIES. GIFTS FASHIONED WITH TIME, ENERGY, AND LOVE ARE THE ONES THAT ARE CHERISHED LONG AFTER THE HUSTLE AND BUSTLE IS OVER. CREATIVE GIFTS SHOW THOSE MOST SPECIAL JUST HOW MUCH YOU APPRECIATE THEM.

MERINGUE SURPRISES
(RECIPE ON PG. 84)

A simple glass jar tied with a ribbon is the perfect container to show off the homemade baked goods inside. Or cut out handmade name tags, and carefully wrap each gift.

MERINGUE SURPRISES
(Photo on page 83)

Makes 10 dozen

4 egg whites
½ teaspoon salt
½ teaspoon cream of tartar
2 teaspoons vanilla extract
1½ cups sugar
1½ cups chopped nuts
1 (12-ounce) package semi-sweet chocolate chips

1. Preheat oven to 350°.

2. Cover cookie sheet with parchment paper.

3. Beat egg whites, salt, cream of tartar, and vanilla extract until soft peaks form.

4. Add sugar gradually, beating until stiff. Fold in nuts and chocolate chips.

5. Drop mixture by teaspoon. Bake 25 minutes.

KAREN'S COCOONS

Makes 5 dozen

1 cup (2 sticks) butter, softened
4 tablespoons powdered sugar
2¼ cups all-purpose flour
2 cups chopped pecans
2 teaspoons vanilla extract
Powdered sugar for coating

1. Preheat oven to 300°.

2. Mix butter with sugar and flour. Add pecans and vanilla extract. Using hands, mix well and shape into walnut-sized balls.

3. Bake on ungreased cookie sheets 30-40 minutes, or until golden. Do not allow to brown.

4. Remove from oven, and roll in powered sugar while warm. When cool, store in airtight container.

HELLO DOLLY BAR COOKIES

Makes 25 pieces

½ cup (1 stick) butter, melted
1 cup graham cracker crumbs
1 cup flaked coconut
1 cup chocolate chips
1 cup chopped pecans
1 (14-ounce) can sweetened condensed milk

1. Preheat oven to 350°.

2. Mix butter and graham cracker crumbs and press firmly into 8-inch square pan. Add flaked coconut, chocolate chips, and pecans, in layers, to completely cover crust.

3. Drizzle sweetened condensed milk over top.

4. Bake 30 minutes. Cool in pan, then cut into squares.

TIP: Cutting is easier if refrigerated for 30 minutes or more.

❦ Like little chronicles of Christmases past, the cookies we bake and share with others each season tell our holiday stories, speak of our cherished family traditions, and, most importantly, remind us what Christmas is really all about.

OATMEAL COOKIES
Makes about 3 dozen

- 1 cup shortening
- ¾ cup sugar
- ¾ cup firmly packed light brown sugar
- 1 egg
- ¼ cup water
- 1 teaspoon vanilla extract
- ½ teaspoon cinnamon
- 1 cup self-rising flour
- 3¼ cups quick cook oatmeal

1. Preheat oven to 350°.

2. Lightly grease cookie sheet.

3. Cream together shortening, sugar, and light brown sugar. Add egg, water, vanilla extract, and cinnamon; beat until smooth. Add flour and blend well. Stir in oatmeal.

4. Drop by teaspoonfuls onto cookie sheet. Bake about 10 minutes. Cookies are done when edges are just beginning to brown, but center still appears doughy.

gifts to
MAKE MEMORIES

Spice of Life

SOME SPICES JUST SMELL LIKE CHRISTMAS AND THE COMFORT AND WARMTH OF HOME. MIX SWEET-SMELLING SPICES FOR HOMEMADE HOLIDAY GIFTS TO SPREAD THE AROMA OF THE SEASON.

A spice-filled aroma in the kitchen can make you feel joyful and sets the tone for guests to arrive with a welcome! Whether it's cinnamon or cardamon, a delicious combination in sweets or beverages pleases the palate. The most traditional spices are cinnamon, nutmeg, allspice, and ginger. All have a warming smell and add a particularly distinct flavor and fragrance to beverages or sweets.

These tartlets are perfect finger food for serving at a party or for boxing up in a creative way to send to loved ones across the street or across the country.

SPICED JAM TARTLETS
(RECIPE ON PG. 88)

SPICED CHOCOLATE TRUFFLES

SPICED CHOCOLATE TRUFFLES

Makes about 48 truffles

12 (1-ounce) squares bittersweet chocolate, chopped
9 (1-ounce) squares semisweet chocolate, chopped
½ teaspoon ground cinnamon
¼ teaspoon chipotle chile powder
½ teaspoon dried orange peel
¼ teaspoon ground cardamom
½ teaspoon finely minced fresh ginger
¼ teaspoon ground ginger
½ cup heavy cream
½ cup whole milk
¼ cup confectioners' sugar
2 (16-ounce) packages chocolate candy coating, melted
Garnish: ground chipotle chile powder, candied orange zest, and candied ginger

1. In a medium bowl, combine the chopped bittersweet and semisweet chocolate. Evenly distribute the chopped chocoalte mixture among 3 small bowls.

2. In one bowl, add cinnamon and chipotle powder. In the second bowl, add the orange zest and cardamom. In the third bowl, add fresh ginger and ground ginger.

3. In medium saucepan, combine the cream, milk, and confectioners' sugar. Bring to a boil, then remove from heat. Evenly divide the hot cream mixture between the 3 bowls of chocolate and spices, whisking gently until chocolate is completely melted. Cover each bowl tightly with plastic wrap; set aside to cool, and then freeze until thoroughly chilled.

4. Line 3 rimmed baking sheets with parchment paper; set aside.

5. Using a 1-inch spring-loaded scoop, scoop chocolate mixture into hands, and roll into a ball. Transfer to prepared baking sheets, keeping each flavor separate. Using two forks, dip truffles into melted candy coating, and place back on the prepared baking sheets. Garnish truffles according to flavor, if desired. Store in an airtight container for up to one week.

SPICED JAM TARTLETS
(Photo on page 87)

Makes 24 bite-size tarts

1 cup all-purpose flour
1 tablespoon sugar
½ teaspoon ground cinnamon
¼ teaspoon ground ginger
¼ teaspoon allspice
⅛ teaspoon salt
¼ cup cream cheese, softened
2 tablespoons unsalted butter, softened
2 tablespoons milk
¾ cup fruit jam, such as fig, pear, or apple
Garnish: dried fruit and raisins

1. In a medium bowl, whisk together the flour, sugar, cinnamon, ginger, allspice, and salt. In a separate medium bowl and using an electric mixer at medium-high speed, beat the cream cheese and buter until smooth and creamy.

2. Reduce mixer speed to low, and slowly add flour mixture and milk to cream cheese mixture; beat until mixture is crumbly. Tranfer dough to a lightly floured surface, form into a disk, and wrap tightly with plastic wrap. Refrigerate for 2 hours.

3. Preheat oven to 350°. Spray 2 (12-cup) mini muffin pans with nonstick cooking spray; set aside.

4. Unwrap dough, and place on a lightly floured surface; knead 3 or 4 times. Divide dough into 24 equal portions, and place 1 piece of dough into each of the muffin wells; pressing into bottoms and up sides.

5. Spoon 1½ teaspoons jam into each dough cup. Bake for 20 minutes, or until crusts are light golden brown. Cool in pans for 10 minutes, then transfer to wire racks to cool completely. Garnish with dried fruit and raisins, if desired.

HOLIDAY TEA

Makes about 1 cup loose-leaf tea for 24 individual servings

2 tablespoons dried orange rind
1 tablespoon dried ginger
24 whole cloves
2 to 4 whole star anise pods
½ cup loose-leaf black tea*

1. In a large bowl, combine the orange rind, ginger, cloves, star anise, and tea leaves; stir well to combine. Place in a decorative bag for gift giving, if desired. If dividing the mixture for several gifts, add a star anise pod to each bag.

*For testing purposes, our test kitchen used Bigelow English Breakfast loose tea.

HOLIDAY TEA

starry anise
The shape of this spice suits the season as an accent in a warm holiday beverage.

CHRISTMAS cottage | 89

festive COOKBOOK

The holidays are for sharing with those we hold most dear. To make events even more memorable, plan menus ahead of time to keep the stress away, and spend the time instead enjoying the fellowship of friends and family.

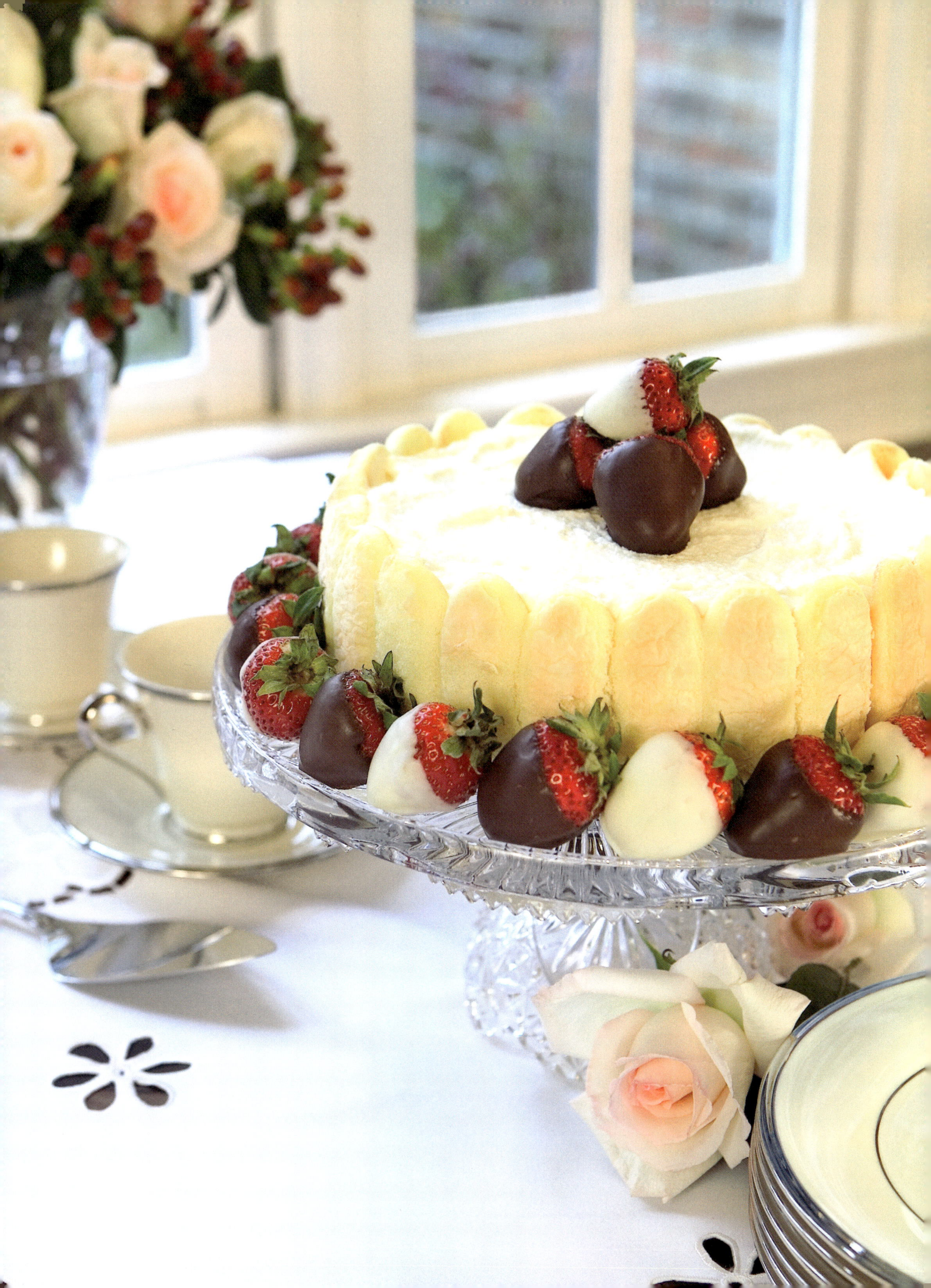

festive
COOKBOOK

Rise & Shine

A PARTICULARLY POPULAR EVENT TO HOST OVER THE HOLIDAY SEASON IS A BRUNCH—WHETHER FOR A GROUP OF FRIENDS ON A WEEKDAY MORNING OR FOR CLOSE-KNIT FAMILY ON CHRISTMAS DAY.

MENU
Cranberry Muffins with Orange Crumble Topping
Herbed Home Fries with Caramelized Onions
Ham, Mushroom, and Spinach Strata
Hot Baked Fruit with Granola Nut Topping
Sparkling Brunch Punch

CRANBERRY MUFFINS WITH ORANGE CRUMBLE TOPPING
(RECIPE ON PG. 95)

92 | CHRISTMAS **cottage**

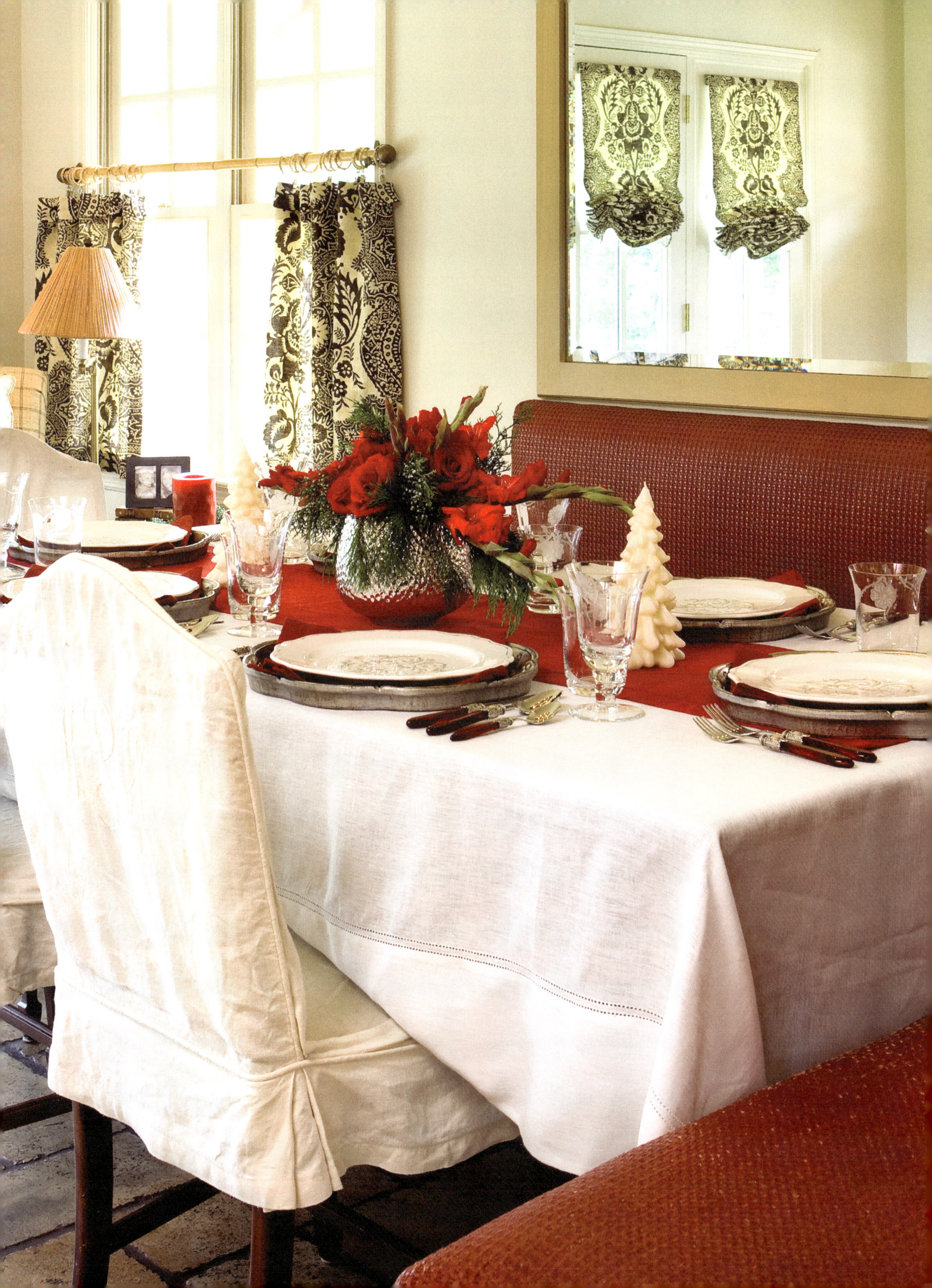

SPARKLING BRUNCH PUNCH

SPARKLING BRUNCH PUNCH

Makes about 1½ gallons

1 (46-ounce) can pineapple juice
6 cups orange juice
1 (12-ounce) can frozen lemonade concentrate, thawed
1 (750-ml) bottle sparkling white grape juice, chilled
1 (2-liter) bottle lemon-lime flavored carbonated beverage, chilled
Garnish: fresh orange slices

1. In a large bowl, combine pineapple juice, orange juice, and lemonade concentrate. When ready to serve, add sparkling white grape juice, and lemon-lime flavored carbonated beverage, stirring gently to combine. Garnish with fresh orange slices, if desired.

CRANBERRY MUFFINS WITH ORANGE CRUMBLE TOPPING
(Photo on page 92)

Makes 1 dozen

1 recipe Orange Crumble Topping (recipe follows)
2 cups all-purpose flour
1 cup sugar
2 teaspoons baking powder
¼ teaspoon salt
1 cup fresh or frozen cranberries
2 large eggs
½ cup butter, melted and cooled
½ cup milk
½ cup sour cream

1. Preheat oven to 400°. Grease and sugar a 12-cup muffin pan; set aside.

2. Prepare Orange Crumble Topping; set aside.

3. In a medium bowl, combine flour, sugar, baking powder, and salt. Add cranberries, stirring to combine.

4. In a separate bowl, whisk together eggs, butter, milk, and sour cream. Add egg mixture to flour mixture, stirring just until dry ingredients are moistened. (Batter will be lumpy; do not over mix.) Evenly divide batter among muffin cups (cups will be almost full). Evenly divide Orange Crumble Topping over top of batter. Bake for 18 to 20 minutes, or until a wooden pick inserted in center comes out clean. Cool in pan for 10 minutes.

ORANGE CRUMBLE TOPPING
Makes ½ cup

¼ cup sugar
¼ cup all-purpose flour
1½ teaspoons grated orange zest
¼ teaspoon ground cinnamon
1 tablespoon butter, melted

1. In a small bowl, combine sugar, flour, orange zest, and cinnamon. Add melted butter, stirring until crumbly.

HERBED HOME FRIES WITH CARAMELIZED ONIONS

Makes 10 to 12 servings

1 (3-pound) bag red skinned potatoes, diced into ¾-inch cubes
10 tablespoons butter, divided
2 large yellow onions, sliced ⅛-inch thick
1 tablespoon balsamic vinegar
1 teaspoon salt, divided
½ teaspoon ground black pepper, divided
1 tablespoon chopped fresh thyme
1 tablespoon chopped fresh parsley
1½ teaspoons chopped fresh rosemary

1. In a Dutch oven, cook potatoes for 3 to 4 minutes in enough boiling salted water to cover. Potatoes should be crisp tender. Drain potatoes, and set aside to cool.

2. In a large nonstick skillet, melt 4 tablespoons butter over medium-high heat. Add onion; cook for 15 minutes, stirring frequently, until caramelized. Add vinegar, ½ teaspoon salt, and ¼ teaspoon pepper; stir until vinegar evaporates, 1 to 2 minutes.

3. Transfer onion mixture to a small bowl.

4. In the same skillet, melt remaining 6 tablespoons butter over medium heat. Add potatoes, pressing them down with a spatula. Cook, without stirring, for 7 to 8 minutes, or until one side is browned. Turn potatoes over with spatula, press down again, and continue to cook for 7 to 8 minutes, without stirring, until well browned. Turn potatoes once more, and cook for an additional 7 to 8 minutes, or until all potatoes are browned and crispy. Stir in reserved onion mixture, remaining ½ teaspoon salt and ¼ teaspoon pepper; thyme, parsley, and rosemary. Serve immediately.

HERBED HOME FRIES WITH CARAMELIZED ONIONS

HOT BAKED FRUIT WITH GRANOLA NUT TOPPING

HOT BAKED FRUIT WITH GRANOLA NUT TOPPING
Makes 10 to 12 servings

- 2 Granny Smith apples, cored and diced
- 2 Braeburn apples, cored and diced
- 2 green D'Anjou pears, cored and diced
- 1 (5-ounce) package dried cherries
- 1 cup firmly packed light brown sugar
- ¼ cup all-purpose flour
- 1 teaspoon ground cinnamon
- 6 tablespoons butter, melted
- 2 cups applesauce
- 1 recipe Granola Nut Topping (recipe follows)

1. Preheat oven to 350°.

2. In a medium bowl, combine apples, pears, and dried cherries.

3. In a separate bowl, combine brown sugar, flour, and cinnamon. Add melted butter to brown sugar mixture, stirring to combine. Add applesauce to brown sugar mixture, stirring to mix well. Combine brown sugar mixture and fruit mixture. Spoon into an ungreased 13x9-inch baking dish. Bake for 45 to 50 minutes, or until fruit is tender. Top with Granola Nut Topping.

GRANOLA NUT TOPPING
Makes about 4½ cups

- 1 cup old-fashioned oats
- ½ cup chopped pecans
- ½ cup slivered almonds
- ½ cup chopped walnuts
- ½ cup sweetened flaked coconut
- 1 teaspoon ground cinnamon
- ¼ cup butter
- 3 tablespoons honey
- 3 tablespoons light brown sugar

1. Preheat oven to 275°. Line a rimmed baking sheet with aluminum foil. Spray foil with nonstick cooking spray; set aside.

2. In a medium bowl, combine oats, pecans, almonds, walnuts, coconut, and cinnamon.

3. In a small saucepan, combine butter, honey, and brown sugar. Bring to a boil over medium heat, stirring until sugar is dissolved. Add butter mixture to oat mixture, stirring to combine well. Spread oat mixture in an even layer on prepared baking sheet. Bake for 35 to 40 minutes, until browned, stirring at 10-minute intervals. Store in an airtight container.

HAM, MUSHROOM, AND SPINACH STRATA
Makes 10 to 12 servings

- 2 tablespoons olive oil
- 1 cup chopped yellow onion
- 1 tablespoon minced garlic
- 1 (8-ounce) package sliced baby portabella mushrooms
- 1 teaspoon salt, divided
- ½ teaspoon ground black pepper, divided
- 6 large eggs
- 1 cup half-and-half
- ½ cup sour cream
- 8 to 10 slices sourdough bread
- 1 (8-ounce) package cream cheese, softened
- 2 cups shredded Monterey Jack Cheese, divided
- ½ pound thinly sliced smoked ham
- 1 (10-ounce) package frozen chopped spinach, thawed and squeezed dry

1. Line a 9-inch square springform pan with heavy-duty aluminum foil. Spray foil with nonstick cooking spray; set aside.

2. In a large skillet, heat olive oil over medium heat. Add onion and garlic; cook for 3 minutes, stirring frequently. Add mushrooms, ½ teaspoon salt, and ¼ teaspoon pepper; cook for 8 minutes, stirring frequently. Set aside to cool.

3. In a medium bowl, whisk together eggs, half-and half, sour cream, remaining ½ teaspoon salt and ¼ teaspoon pepper.

4. Layer half of bread slices in bottom of prepared springform pan. Continue with half of cream cheese, ¾ cup Monterey Jack cheese, half of ham, half of spinach, and half of mushroom mixture. Slowly pour half of egg mixture over layered strata. Repeat layers for remaining bread, cream cheese, ¾ cup Monterey Jack cheese, ham, spinach, mushroom mixture and egg mixture. Top with remaining ½ cup Monterey Jack cheese. Cover and refrigerate for at least 1 hour, or overnight, if desired.

5. Remove from refrigerator, and let come to room temperature before baking.

6. Preheat oven to 350°.

7. Bake for 1 hour to 1 hour 5 minutes, or until browned and set. Cool strata for 15 minutes before serving.

HAM, MUSHROOM, AND SPINACH STRATA

festive
COOKBOOK

Christmas Buffet Style

WHEN THE HOUSE IS FULL OF THOSE MOST DEAR, IT'S IMPORTANT TO CATCH UP AND SPEND QUALITY TIME WITH ONE ANOTHER. A BUFFET-STYLE CHRISTMAS IS A PRACTICAL WAY TO ENJOY THE GATHERING.

MENU
Sausage Breakfast Casserole
Hot Curried Fruit
Double Cheese Grits Casserole
Sweet Potato Pecan Muffins
Cranberry Splash

✤ A buffet-style Christmas meal is casual and conversational, making the day much more relaxed for the host. Although it takes just as much work to plan, a buffet allows the host time to mix and mingle with guests.

CRANBERRY SPLASH

Makes 1 gallon

8 cups cranberry juice cocktail, chilled
8 cups pineapple-orange juice, chilled

1. Combine all ingredients in a large pitcher, stirring well. Serve over ice, if desired.

SAUSAGE BREAKFAST CASSEROLE

Makes 8 servings

1 (8-ounce) can refrigerator crescent rolls
1 pound ground pork sausage
1 cup shredded Cheddar cheese
1 cup shredded mozzarella cheese
6 eggs, lightly beaten
1½ cups milk
½ teaspoon salt
Garnish: tomato wedges

1. Preheat oven to 375°.

2. Unroll crescent rolls. Place in bottom of a lightly greased 13 x 9 x 2-inch baking dish, pressing perforations together to form a crust. Bake for 6 minutes. (Crust will be puffy.) Remove from oven and set aside. Reduce oven temperature to 350°.

3. In a large skillet, brown sausage, stirring to crumble into small pieces. Drain, spoon over baked crust, then sprinkle with cheeses.

4. Combine eggs, milk, and salt; pour over the sausage and cheese. Bake at 350° for 35 to 40 minutes (until top is golden brown).

HOT CURRIED FRUIT

Makes 10 servings

1 (29-ounce) can peach halves, drained
1 (29-ounce) can pear halves, drained
1 (20-ounce) can pineapple chunks, drained
1 (15¼-ounce) can apricot halves, drained
1 (6-ounce) jar maraschino cherries without stems, drained
½ cup butter or margarine, melted
¾ cup firmly packed brown sugar
2 tablespoons all-purpose flour
1 teaspoon curry powder

1. Preheat oven to 350°.

2. Combine fruit in a large bowl. Pour melted butter over fruit. Combine brown sugar, flour, and curry powder; add to fruit, stirring gently. Spoon mixture into a lightly greased 13 x 9 x 2-inch baking dish. Cover and bake for 30 minutes or until thoroughly heated.

SWEET POTATO PECAN MUFFINS

Makes 14 muffins

1⅔ cups all-purpose flour
1 teaspoon baking soda
¼ teaspoon baking powder
¾ teaspoon salt
¾ teaspoon ground cinnamon
¼ teaspoon ground nutmeg
½ cup chopped pecans
⅓ cup shortening
1⅓ cups sugar
2 large eggs
1 (15-ounce) can sweet potatoes, drained and mashed
⅓ cup water

1. Preheat oven to 350°.

2. Combine first 7 ingredients in a large bowl; make a well in center of mixture.

3. In a mixing bowl, beat shortening at medium speed of an electric mixer until creamy; gradually add sugar, beating well. Add eggs, one at a time, beating after each addition. Add mashed sweet potatoes and water, beating well. Add to dry ingredients; stir just until moistened.

4. Spoon batter into 14 greased muffin pans. Bake for 20 to 25 minutes. Remove from pans immediately and cool on wire racks.

DOUBLE CHEESE GRITS CASSEROLE

Makes 8 servings

2½ cups milk
2 cups water
½ teaspoon salt
1 cup regular grits, uncooked
2 cups (8 ounces) shredded Cheddar cheese
½ cup butter or margarine
½ cup grated Parmesan cheese
2 large eggs
Paprika

1. Preheat oven to 350°.

2. Combine milk, water, and salt in a large saucepan; bring to a boil. Stir in grits. Cover, reduce heat, and simmer 15 minutes, stirring occasionally. Add Cheddar cheese, butter and Parmesan cheese. Stir until cheese and butter melt.

3. In a small bowl, beat eggs with a fork. Into the eggs, gradually stir in a small amount of the hot grits mixture, then stir this back into the grits mixture in the saucepan. Pour into a lightly greased 2-quart baking dish. Sprinkle with paprika. Bake, uncovered, for 40 to 45 minutes.

festive
COOKBOOK

Turkey Tradition

CHRISTMAS IS THE SEASON OF SHARING AND CELEBRATING. AND THERE'S NO BETTER WAY THAN TO HOST A CASUAL DINNER PARTY.

MENU

Holiday Italian Salad
Deep-Fried Turkey
Cornbread Dressing
Squash & Zucchini Casserole
Broccoli & Cheese Stuffed Potatoes
Glazed Carrots
Easy Orange Rolls
White-Chocolate Mousse Cake

This menu features Deep-Fried Turkey conveniently cooked outdoors, leaving the kitchen as the primary area for preparing all the trimmings. Make the Holiday Italian Salad and White-Chocolate Mousse Cake a day in advance to make hosting the affair less hectic.

HOLIDAY ITALIAN SALAD
Makes 8 servings

4 cups torn green-leaf lettuce
4 cups torn red-leaf lettuce
1 cup chopped walnuts, toasted
1 yellow bell pepper, cut into thin strips
1 orange bell pepper, cut into thin strips
1 recipe Creamy Balsamic Italian Dressing (recipe follows)

1. In a large bowl, combine all ingredients except dressing. Add dressing, tossing gently. Serve immediately.

CREAMY BALSAMIC ITALIAN DRESSING
Makes about 2 cups

1 (.7-ounce) envelope zesty Italian salad-dressing mix
3 tablespoons water
¼ cup balsamic vinegar
½ cup olive oil
1 cup commercial ranch dressing

1. Combine all ingredients in a small bowl; whisk until well blended. Cover and chill for 1 hour. Whisk well before serving.

on the rise
Since the oven will be working overtime leading up to this special meal, try proofing Easy Orange Rolls away from the hectic activity of the kitchen. Clear off a small table in another room, and cover it with an electric blanket. Turn the blanket on low for 10 minutes, then turn it off. Place the pans of rolls on the warm blanket, and let the rolls rise in this undisturbed room.

HOLIDAY ITALIAN SALAD

EASY ORANGE ROLLS
Makes 36 rolls

6 tablespoons butter, melted
3 tablespoons fresh orange juice
1 teaspoon grated orange zest
1 (3-pound) package frozen roll dough, thawed
1 recipe Orange Glaze (recipe follows)

1. Stir together melted butter, orange juice, and zest; set aside.

2. Grease 36 muffin cups.

3. Divide each roll into 3 equal parts; roll into balls. Dip each ball into butter mixture. Place 3 balls into each muffin cup. Cover, and let rise in a warm place, free from drafts, until doubled in bulk, for approximately 2 hours.

4. Preheat oven to 350°. Bake for 10 to 12 minutes, or until lightly browned. Drizzle with glaze.

ORANGE GLAZE
Makes about 1 cup

1½ cups powdered sugar
3 tablespoons fresh orange juice

1. Combine all ingredients, stirring until smooth.

SQUASH & ZUCCHINI CASSEROLE
Makes 12 to 16 servings

½ cup plus 2 tablespoons butter or margarine, divided
6 medium zucchini, thinly sliced
4 medium yellow squash, thinly sliced
1 (8-ounce) package sliced fresh mushrooms
1 onion, chopped
1 teaspoon salt
1 teaspoon ground black pepper
1 sleeve round butter crackers, crushed
½ cup grated Parmesan cheese

1. In a large skillet over medium-high heat on stovetop, melt ½ cup butter. Add vegetables; cook, uncovered, for 20 minutes, or until tender; stirring often. Add salt and pepper.

2. Preheat oven to 350°.

3. Spoon squash mixture into a 9-x-13-x-2-inch baking dish; set aside.

4. In a medium saucepan over low heat on stovetop, melt remaining 2 tablespoons butter. Remove from heat. Stir in crushed crackers and cheese. Sprinkle mixture over casserole.

5. Bake for 45 minutes.

CHRISTMAS cottage | 101

BROCCOLI & CHEESE STUFFED POTATOES

Makes 10 servings

10 large baking potatoes
1 (16-ounce) carton sour cream
1 (8-ounce) package cream cheese, softened
¼ cup butter
2 teaspoons salt
1 teaspoon ground black pepper
3 cups fresh broccoli florets, cooked until crisp-tender
1 cup shredded Colby-Jack cheese blend

1. Preheat oven to 425°.

2. Wash potatoes and wrap potatoes in foil. Place on a baking sheet. Bake for 1 hour, or until done. Cool potatoes until easy to handle.

3. Cut off top third of potatoes lengthwise, and scoop out pulp, leaving ¼-inch-thick shells.

4. Preheat oven to 350°.

5. In a large bowl, mash potato pulp. Add sour cream and next 4 ingredients, stirring until well blended. Add cooked broccoli, stirring gently. Spoon potato-broccoli mixture into potato shells.

6. Place potatoes on a baking sheet. Bake for 30 minutes. Sprinkle tops with shredded cheese. Bake for 10

DEEP-FRIED TURKEY

Makes 1 (13-pound) turkey

2 teaspoons dried oregano
2 teaspoons dried basil
1 teaspoon dried parsley
1 teaspoon salt
1 teaspoon ground black pepper
1 (13-pound) turkey
3 to 4 gallons peanut oil
Garnish: fresh parsley and sage

1. Combine first 5 ingredients; set aside.

2. Remove giblets and neck from turkey. Remove plastic ring holding legs together and pop-up timer. Rinse turkey with cold water and pat dry. Loosen skin from breast without detaching it; carefully rub spice mixture under skin. Let stand 30 minutes before frying.

3. Heat peanut oil in propane turkey fryer to 375° over medium-low flame, following manufacturer's instructions. (See page 25 for step-by-step photos.) Place turkey in fryer basket. Carefully lower basket into hot oil. Temperature should fall and remain at 325°. Cook for approximately 45 minutes (3½ minutes per pound at 325°). Slowly remove basket from oil. Drain and cool slightly before slicing.

4. If desired, garnish with fresh parsley and sage.

FRIED TURKEY IS A DELICIOUS SOUTHERN TRADITION THAT JUST HAPPENS TO BE EASY, TOO. HOWEVER, THERE ARE A FEW SAFETY TIPS TO KEEP IN MIND:

- *Always fry outdoors.*
- *Never leave frying turkey unattended.*
- *Have a fire extinguisher handy.*
- *Allow oil to cool completely before moving fryer.*

STEP-BY-STEP

[1] Place turkey in fryer basket, lower basket into fryer, and fill with peanut oil to 1-inch above turkey.

[2] Remove turkey in fryer basket and let drain on pan covered with paper towels. Light propane burner.

[3] Heat oil to 375° over medium-low flame. This will take 30 to 45 minutes.

[4] Using an oven mitt and the fryer hook, very slowly lower fryer basket with turkey into hot oil to avoid spillage.

[5] Cover fryer and insert thermometer in lid. Temperature should drop and remain at 325°. Adjust propane flame as needed to maintain temperature.

[6] Fry turkey for 3½ minutes per pound. Meat thermometer inserted in thigh should reach 180°. To avoid starting a fire, turn off propane before removing turkey from fryer. Using an oven mitt and the fryer hook, very slowly lift fryer basket. Drain over fryer.

GLAZED CARROTS

Makes 8 to 12 servings

2 pounds baby carrots
3 tablespoons butter
½ cup brown sugar
¼ cup fresh orange juice
2 teaspoons cornstarch
½ teaspoon grated orange zest
¼ teaspoon ground ginger
¼ teaspoon salt

1. In a large saucepan, cover carrots with water. Bring to a boil over high heat on stovetop. Reduce heat to low and cover. Cook for 10 minutes, or until tender. Drain well. Set aside, and keep warm.

2. In a small saucepan, combine butter and next 5 ingredients. Cook over medium heat on stovetop, stirring constantly, until mixture boils. Boil for 1 minute, stirring constantly. Remove from heat; stir in salt. Pour mixture over carrots; toss well.

CORNBREAD DRESSING

Makes 12 to 16 servings

2 (6-ounce) packages buttermilk cornbread mix
½ cup butter
2 cups chopped onion
2 cups chopped celery
2 cups crumbled biscuits
1 tablespoon poultry seasoning
1 teaspoon salt
4½ cups chicken broth
1 (10.75-ounce) can cream of chicken soup
3 eggs, beaten

1. Prepare and bake cornbread mix according to package directions. Cool, and crumble; set aside.

2. Preheat oven to 350°.

3. In a large skillet over medium-high heat on stovetop, melt butter. Add onion and celery; cook, stirring constantly, for 7 minutes, or until tender.

4. In a large bowl, combine crumbled cornbread, crumbled biscuits, poultry seasoning, and salt; stir in vegetable mixture. Add broth, soup, and eggs, stirring well. Pour mixture into a lightly greased 9-x-13-x-2-inch baking dish. Bake for 45 to 50 minutes, or until center is set.

WHITE-CHOCOLATE MOUSSE CAKE

It's important to thoroughly dry strawberries before dipping in melted chocolate. Refrigerate the chocolate-dipped strawberries up to 24 hours, but for optimum flavor, let them stand at room temperature before garnishing the cake.

WHITE-CHOCOLATE MOUSSE CAKE

Makes 1 (9-inch) cake

2 (3-ounce) packages ladyfingers, split
¾ cup milk
30 large marshmallows
6 (1-ounce) squares white baking chocolate
1 pint whipping cream
1 recipe Strawberry Sauce (recipe follows)
Garnish: chocolate-dipped strawberries

1. Line bottom and sides of a 9-inch springform pan with ladyfingers; set aside.

2. In a heavy saucepan, combine milk, marshmallows, and chocolate. Cook over low heat on stovetop, stirring constantly, until smooth. Remove from heat. Cool for 20 minutes.

3. Beat whipping cream at high speed with an electric mixer until soft peaks form. Gently fold into cooled chocolate mixture.

4. Pour chocolate mixture into prepared pan. Cover and chill for at least 4 hours. Serve with Strawberry Sauce.

5. If desired, garnish with chocolate-dipped strawberries.

STRAWBERRY SAUCE

Makes 1½ cups

1 (10-ounce) package frozen sliced strawberries, thawed
2 teaspoons cornstarch
½ cup light corn syrup
1 teaspoon lemon juice

1. In a small saucepan, combine all ingredients. Cook over medium heat on stovetop, stirring constantly, until mixture boils. Boil for 1 minute, stirring constantly. Remove from heat; cool before serving.

festive
COOKBOOK

Tiny Appetizers

KEEP THE OFFERINGS ON THE SMALL SIDE FOR HOLIDAY COMPANY. FROM A TINY SCONE TO A PETITE SHRIMP CUP, FRIENDS AND FAMILY WILL ENJOY THESE DELIGHTFUL RECIPES.

MENU
Shrimp Mousse with Saffron Aïoli in Phyllo Cups
Roasted Beef Finger Sandwiches with Kalamata Mustard Butter
Honey Scones with Apricot Preserves
Brandy Cream in Chocolate Cups
Lemon Glazed Miniature Cakes

BRANDY CREAM IN CHOCOLATE CUPS
(RECIPE ON PG. 106)

ROASTED BEEF FINGER SANDWICHES WITH KALAMATA MUSTARD BUTTER

SHRIMP MOUSSE WITH SAFFRON AÏOLI IN PHYLLO CUPS

ROASTED BEEF FINGER SANDWICHES WITH KALAMATA MUSTARD BUTTER

Makes 15 sandwiches

½ cup butter, softened
½ cup chopped Kalamata olives
¼ cup deli-style mustard
1 tablespoon chopped fresh Italian parsley
⅛ teaspoon ground black pepper
5 slices wheat bread, crusts removed
5 slices white bread, crusts removed
¼ pound thinly sliced deli roast beef
Garnish: blanched chives, Italian parsley, and pimiento

1. Using food processor, combine butter, olives, mustard, Italian parsley, and pepper. Pulse until mixture is combined but still chunky.

2. Spread butter mixture on wheat bread slices; top white bread slices with thinkly sliced roast beef. Place remaining bread slices on top of roast beef.

3. Cut into fingers. Garnish by wrapping each with blanched chive, and tie in knot. Trim ends of chives if necessary. Tuck Italian parsley and pimiento in center of tie, if desired.

SHRIMP MOUSSE WITH SAFFRON AÏOLI IN PHYLLO CUPS

Makes 30 shells

½ pound large fresh shrimp, cooked
1 (8-ounce) package cream cheese, softened
½ cup butter, softened
1 clove garlic, minced
1 tablespoon minced fresh chives
2 (2.1-ounce) packages frozen phyllo shells, thawed
Saffron Aïoli (recipe follows)
Garnish: baby shrimp

1. Peel and devein shrimp.

2. Using food processor, combine cream cheese, butter, garlic, and chives. Pulse until combined. Add shrimp and pulse until shrimp are coarsely chopped.

3. Spoon mixture into phyllo shells. Drizzle with saffron aioli. Garnish with baby shrimp, if desired.

SAFFRON AÏOLI
Makes about ½ cup

½ cup mayonnaise
2 tablespoons heavy cream
½ teaspoon Dijon mustard
Pinch saffron
1 clove garlic, minced

1. In small bowl, combine mayonnaise, cream, mustard, saffron, and garlic. Mix well.

HONEY SCONES WITH APRICOT PRESERVES

BRANDY CREAM IN CHOCOLATE CUPS
(photo pg. 104)

Makes 36 cordial cups

2 cups heavy cream
½ cup confectioners' sugar
3 tablespoons brandy
3 (3.15-ounce) boxes molded chocolate cordial cups
Thinly sliced strawberries
Sugared Almonds (recipe follows)

1. In medium bowl and using electric mixer at medium speed, beat cream until thickened.

2. Add confectioners' sugar, 1 tablespoon at a time, beating continually until stiff peaks form. Stir in brandy.

3. Spoon brandy cream into chocolate cordial cups. Place each cup on strawberry slice, and sprinkle with Sugared Almonds.

SUGARED ALMONDS
Makes about ½ cup

2 tablespoons butter
½ cup sliced almonds
2 tablespoons sugar

1. In small skillet, melt butter over medium heat.

2. Stir in almonds, and cook until lightly browned. Add sugar, stirring to coat. Spoon mixture onto wax paper to cool.

HONEY SCONES WITH APRICOT PRESERVES

Makes 15 scones

2¼ cups all-purpose flour
¼ cup sugar
2½ teaspoons baking powder
¾ teaspoon ground ginger
¼ teaspoon salt
½ cup butter
¼ cup honey
½ cup plus 1 tablespoon heavy cream
Sparkling sugar

1. Preheat oven to 350°.

2. Lightly grease baking sheet.

3. In large bowl, combine flour, sugar, baking powder, ginger, and salt. Using pastry blender, cut in butter until mixture is crumbly.

4. In small bowl, combine honey and ½ cup cream. Add to dry ingredients, stirring just until moistened.

5. On lightly floured surface, roll dough to ½-inch thickness. Using 3-inch cutter, cut scones and place on baking sheet; brush with 1 tablespoon cream and sprinkle with sparkling sugar. Bake 18 to 20 minutes, or until lightly browned.

APRICOT PRESERVES
Makes 4½ cups

3 cups finely chopped dried apricots
3 cups water
2 cups sugar

1. Combine apricots, water, and sugar in slow cooker.

2. Cook, covered, on high 3½ hours, stirring occasionally.

3. Uncover and cook 1 hour, stirring occasionally. Cover and chill.

delicate dipped apricots

You can prepare chocolate dipped apricots fairly easily, and they make neat little additions to the Christmas table. Take a package of dried apricots, dip each halfway in melted candy bark. Lay on a waxed-paper-lined pan and cool in the refrigerator for an hour. You may add a tablespoon of brandy to flavor the bark a bit if you like a little kick in the chocolate.

LEMON GLAZED MINIATURE CAKES

Makes 36 tea cakes

- 1 cup butter
- 1¾ cups sugar
- 2 large eggs
- 1 teaspoon vanilla extract
- 3½ cups all-purpose flour
- 1 teaspoon baking soda
- 1 teaspoon cream of tartar
- ¾ cup plus 2 tablespoons buttermilk
- ¾ cup plus 2 tablespoons confectioners' sugar
- 2 tablespoons fresh lemon juice

1. Preheat oven to 350°.
2. Lightly grease mini muffin pans.
3. In large bowl and using electric mixer, beat butter and sugar until fluffy. Add eggs, one at a time, beating well after each addition. Stir in vanilla extract.
4. In medium bowl, combine flour, baking soda, and cream of tartar. Add to butter mixture alternately with buttermilk, beginning and ending with flour.
5. Spoon batter into mini muffin pans, filling ¾ full. Bake 15 to 18 minutes or until done. Immediately remove tea cakes to wire racks.
6. In small bowl, combine confectioners' sugar and lemon juice. Brush cooled tea cakes with lemon glaze.

festive
COOKBOOK

Bits of Flavor

MANY PARTIES THIS TIME OF YEAR CATER TO CROWDS WHO LIKE TO WALK AROUND THE ROOM TO MIX AND MINGLE, SO FINGER FOODS AND COCKTAILS ARE OFTEN THE MENU OF CHOICE.

❈ A full dinner menu is not necessary when appetizers are hearty and full of flavor. Finger foods are easy for partygoers to pick up and nibble on as they visit with friends.

—Adapted from *Porch Parties* by Denise Gee, and published by Chronicle Books.

RUBY SANGRIA

CHERRY TOMATOES WITH JALAPEÑO-PIMIENTO CHEESE
Serves 8 to 12

About 2 dozen large cherry or small Roma tomatoes
Jalapeño-Pimiento Cheese (recipe follows)
Garnish: Jalapeño slivers (optional)

1. Remove the stems, then cut the tomatoes in half width-wise. Use melon baller or teaspoon to gently scoop out pulp. Place upside down on paper towels to drain.

2. Using a teaspoon, gently stuff Jalapeno-Pimiento Cheese into each tomato half. Garnish, if desired.

JALAPEÑO-PIMIENTO CHEESE
Makes 4 cups

1 small white onion, chopped
3 cloves garlic
1 or 2 jalapeños, de-seeded, stems removed, chopped
½ pound medium yellow cheddar cheese, grated
½ pound white sharp cheddar cheese, grated
1 7-ounce jar pimientos, drained
1 cup mayonnaise
White pepper

1. In a food processor, finely chop the onion, garlic, and jalapeño(s).

2. Place the cheeses and pimientos in a medium bowl. Add the vegetables and mayonnaise and mix well. Season with white pepper.

ASPARAGUS-PROSCIUTTO PUFFS
Makes 24 puffs

24 small to medium (not thin) asparagus spears
1 17.3-ounce package frozen puff pastry, thawed
1 5.2-ounce package Boursin or herbed cream cheese
12 slices of prosciutto, halved

CHERRY TOMATOES WITH JALAPEÑO-PIMIENTO CHEESE

ASPARAGUS-PROSCIUTTO PUFFS

1. Preheat oven to 400 degrees F.

2. Trim asparagus to 5 to 6 inches in length.

3. Place the asparagus in a pot of boiling water until crisp-tender, about 3 minutes. Remove from the water with slotted spoon and drain.

4. Spread out both puff pastry portions and slice both in half vertically, making 4 sections. Slice each section horizontally into six equal-size strips about 3 inches wide by 2 inches long.

5. Spread ½ teaspoon cheese onto each pastry strip, avoiding the edges, and top with prosciutto slice, folded to fit atop cheese. Add one asparagus spear at the top of prosciutto and cheese and roll into a slim bundle, pinching the dough together to firmly seal.

6. Place the pastry bundles seam-side down onto a nonstick baking sheet lined with parchment paper. (Do not use a greased baking sheet or the bundle will be soggy.) Bake until the bundles are puffed and golden, about 10 minutes. Place on wire racks to cool slightly before serving.

RUBY SANGRIA
Serves 6 to 8

1 750-milliliter bottle red wine
½ cup brandy
½ cup orange-flavored liqueur
½ cup fresh orange juice
¼ cup sugar
2 cups orange wedges
2 cups red apple wedges
2 cups green apple wedges
2 cups grapes
1 750-millileter bottle sparkling water, chilled
Garnish: Grapes and orange wedges, red and green apple wedges (about 1 cup each) threaded on small wooden skewers (optional)

1. Combine the red wine, brandy, liqueur, orange juice, and sugar in large pitcher or plastic container; stir well. Add the oranges, red and green apples, and grapes. Chill for several hours.

2. Just before serving, add the sparkling water.

3. Pour the sangria into red-wine goblets or cocktail glasses filled with ice. Garnish with fruit kebobs, if desired.

festive
COOKBOOK

Ornament Swap Party

ADDING A TOUCH OF SPARKLE AND CHARACTER TO YOUR CHRISTMAS TREE NEVER GETS OLD. THAT'S WHY ORNAMENT SWAPS ARE ALWAYS A BIG HIT—ESPECIALLY WHEN DELICIOUS TREATS AND SNACKS ARE SERVED DURING THE FESTIVITIES.

MENU
Prosciutto and Brie Dip
Mini Potato Skins with Horseradish Dipping Sauce
Pizza Rolls with Marinara Sauce
Pecan Pie Tartlets
Kahlúa and Coffee Fudge
Amaretto Cheesecake Squares
Hot Rum Punch

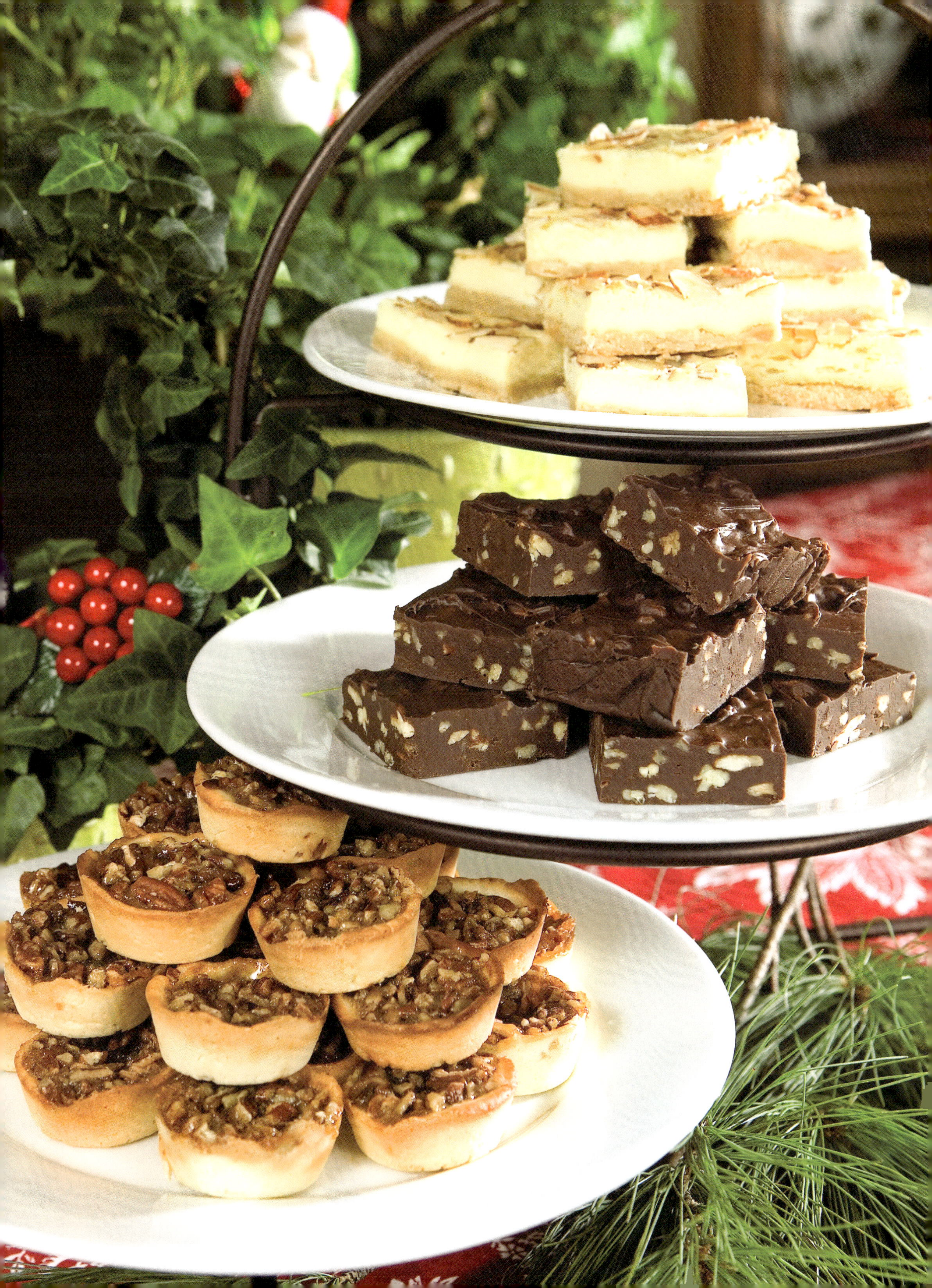

PROSCIUTTO AND BRIE DIP
Makes 10 to 12 servings

1 cup sour cream
1 (8-ounce) package cream cheese, softened
3 (5-ounce) containers crème de brie*
½ cup grated Parmesan cheese
1½ cups chopped prosciutto, (about 6 ounces)
¼ cup chopped green onion
½ teaspoon red pepper flakes

1. Preheat oven to 375°. In a large bowl, combine sour cream, cream cheese, crème de brie, and Parmesan cheese. Beat at medium speed with electric mixer until smooth. Add prosciutto, green onion, and red pepper flakes, beating to combine. Spoon mixture into an 8-inch square baking dish. Bake 15 to 20 minutes, or until bubbly. Serve with crackers or Melba toast rounds.

*If crème de brie is not available, 15 ounces of softened brie with rind removed may be substituted.

MINI POTATO SKINS WITH HORSERADISH DIPPING SAUCE
Makes 2 dozen

12 small red potatoes, washed and dried
3 tablespoons olive oil, divided
1 teaspoon Creole seasoning
½ teaspoon salt
¼ teaspoon ground black pepper
1½ cups shredded Cheddar and Monterey Jack cheese blend
8 slices bacon, cooked and crumbled
¼ cup chopped green onion
1 recipe Horseradish Dipping Sauce (recipe follows)

1. Preheat oven to 375°. Line a baking sheet with aluminum foil. Rub potatoes with 1 tablespoon olive oil to coat skins. Place on prepared baking sheet. Bake 45 minutes or until done.

2. Cool potatoes until easy to handle. Cut potatoes in half; using a teaspoon or melon baller, scoop out pulp, leaving ¼-inch-thick shells. Discard potato pulp or reserve for another use.

3. In a small bowl, combine 2 tablespoons olive oil, Creole seasoning, salt, and pepper. Brush inside of potatoes with olive oil mixture. Bake 15 minutes. Top with cheese, bacon, and green onion; bake 5 minutes, or until cheese is melted. Serve with Horseradish Dipping Sauce.

HORSERADISH DIPPING SAUCE
Makes 1½ cups

1 cup sour cream
½ cup mayonnaise
2 tablespoons prepared horseradish
1 tablespoon chopped fresh chives
¼ teaspoon salt
¼ teaspoon ground black pepper

1. Combine all ingredients in a small bowl. Cover and chill until ready to serve.

PIZZA ROLLS WITH MARINARA SAUCE
Makes 1 dozen

2 tablespoons olive oil
1 cup chopped fresh mushrooms

PIZZA ROLLS WITH MARINARA SAUCE

PECAN PIE TARTLETS

½ cup chopped onion
¼ cup chopped red bell pepper
½ teaspoon salt
¼ teaspoon ground black pepper
6 cloves garlic, minced
½ pound Italian sausage, cooked and crumbled
1 cup chopped pepperoni
1 (12-ounce) can tomato paste
1 cup shredded Italian blend cheese
12 egg roll wrappers
1 large egg, lightly beaten
Vegetable oil for frying
1 recipe Marinara Sauce (recipe follows)

1. In a large sauté pan, heat olive oil over medium heat. Add mushrooms, onion, red pepper, salt, and pepper. Cook 4 to 5 minutes or until vegetables are tender. Add garlic and cook 1 minute. Add sausage, pepperoni, and tomato paste, stirring to mix well. Cook 2 to 3 minutes, stirring constantly. Remove from heat and cool slightly; stir in cheese.

2. Spoon 2 tablespoons filling on bottom one-third of egg roll wrapper. Fold the lower corner over filling, and roll it up about one-third of the way. Brush the left and right corners of wrapper with beaten egg; fold corners toward center of filling. Brush top edge with egg and roll up tightly; repeat for each roll.

3. Fill a Dutch oven with 2 inches of oil; heat to 350°. Fry pizza rolls, in batches, 3 to 4 minutes, or until golden brown. Drain on paper towels.

MARINARA SAUCE
Makes 2½ cups

1 tablespoon olive oil
3 cloves garlic, minced
1 (28-ounce) can crushed tomatoes
1 tablespoon Italian seasoning
1 teaspoon sugar
½ teaspoon salt
¼ teaspoon ground black pepper

1. In a medium saucepan, heat olive oil over medium heat. Add garlic and cook 1 minute. Add tomatoes and remaining ingredients, stirring to combine. Reduce heat to low and simmer uncovered 20 minutes. Serve warm.

PECAN PIE TARTLETS
Makes about 3 dozen

CRUST:
½ cup sugar
¼ cup butter, softened
1 (3-ounce) package cream cheese, softened
1 large egg
1¾ cups all-purpose flour

FILLING:
⅓ cup light corn syrup
⅓ cup dark corn syrup
½ cup sugar
2 tablespoons butter, melted
2 large eggs, lightly beaten
1 teaspoon vanilla extract
¾ cup finely chopped pecans

1. In a medium bowl, combine ½ cup sugar, ¼ cup butter, and cream cheese. Beat at medium speed with an electric mixer until smooth. Add one egg, beating until smooth. Gradually add flour. Beat at low speed until just combined; dough will be sticky. Cover and chill dough 1 hour.

(continued on next page)

KAHLÚA AND COFFEE FUDGE

AMARETTO CHEESECAKE SQUARES

2. Roll dough into 1-inch balls; press in bottom and two-thirds up sides of each cup of a miniature muffin pan. Preheat oven to 350°. In a medium bowl, combine corn syrup, ½ cup sugar, melted butter, 2 eggs, and vanilla, whisking to combine. Spoon corn syrup mixture into each prepared crust. Top with chopped pecans. Bake 18 to 20 minutes, or until lightly browned.

KAHLÚA AND COFFEE FUDGE
Makes 10 to 12 servings

- 1 (14-ounce) can sweetened condensed milk
- ¼ cup Kahlúa
- 2 tablespoons instant coffee granules
- 1 (12-ounce) package semisweet chocolate morsels
- 1 cup chopped pecans
- ½ teaspoon vanilla extract

1. Line an 8-inch square baking pan with aluminum foil. In a large, heavy-duty saucepan, combine condensed milk, Kahlúa, and coffee granules over medium heat. Bring to a simmer; cook 2 minutes, stirring constantly, until mixture thickens slightly. Remove from heat and stir in chocolate morsels, until melted and smooth. Stir in pecans and vanilla.

2. Spread evenly into prepared baking pan. Refrigerate 2 hours. Remove from pan by lifting foil. Peel back foil and cut into squares to serve.

AMARETTO CHEESECAKE SQUARES
Makes 2 dozen

- 1¾ cups all-purpose flour, divided
- ½ cup firmly packed light brown sugar
- ½ cup butter, melted
- 2 (8-ounce) packages cream cheese, softened
- ½ cup sugar
- 4 large eggs
- ¼ cup amaretto liqueur
- ½ teaspoon almond extract
- ⅓ cup sliced almonds

1. Preheat oven to 350°. Combine 1½ cups flour, brown sugar, and melted butter. Press firmly in bottom of a 13x9x2-inch baking pan. Bake 6 to 8 minutes.

2. In a large bowl, combine cream cheese, sugar, and ¼ cup flour. Beat at medium speed with an electric mixer, until well combined. Add eggs, one at a time, beating well after each addition. Add amaretto and almond extract, beating to combine.

3. Spread filling over prepared crust; sprinkle with sliced almonds. Bake 25 minutes, or until set. Cool completely. Cover and refrigerate 2 hours to overnight; cut into squares.

OPPOSITE: This hot rum drink garnished with clove-studded citrus slices and served in polka-dotted tumblers packs a delightful punch.

HOT RUM PUNCH
Makes about 3 quarts

1 (64-ounce) bottle apple cider
½ cup sugar
3 cinnamon sticks
1 tablespoon whole cloves
2 cups fresh orange juice
1 cup light rum
½ cup fresh lemon juice
Garnish: fresh orange slices

1. In a Dutch oven over medium heat, combine apple cider, sugar, cinnamon sticks, and cloves. Simmer uncovered for 10 minutes; remove spices and discard. Add orange juice, rum, and lemon juice. Garnish with fresh orange slices, if desired.

festive
COOKBOOK

By the Fireside

WHEN THE CHILL WINDS OF WINTER BLOW, CURLING UP IN FRONT OF A FIREPLACE IS A PAMPERING PLEASURE THAT IS IMPOSSIBLE TO RESIST.

MENU
Creamy Herbed Spinach Soup
Ham & Jarlsberg Sandwiches
Roast Beef Roll-Ups with Maytag Blue Cheese & Caramelized Onions
Gingerbread Fingers with Orange Crème Filling
Dark Chocolate Raspberry Mousse Cake

HAM & JARLSBERG SANDWICHES (RECIPE ON PG. 117)
ROAST BEEF ROLL-UPS WITH MAYTAG BLUE CHEESE AND CARAMELIZED ONIONS (RECIPE ON PG. 118)

CREAMY HERBED SPINACH SOUP

Makes 5 cups

2 tablespoons olive oil
1 small onion, chopped
2 cloves garlic, minced
2 cups chicken broth
1 (12-ounce) package fresh baby spinach, washed
2 tablespoons chopped fresh basil
2 tablespoons chopped fresh parsley
1 cup heavy cream
½ cup sour cream
⅓ cup grated Parmesan cheese
½ teaspoon salt
½ teaspoon ground black pepper
Garnish: croutons, shredded Parmesan cheese

1. In Dutch oven over medium-high heat, heat olive oil. Sauté onion until tender; add garlic and sauté 1 to 2 minutes.

2. Add chicken broth and spinach. Bring to boil, reduce heat, cover, and simmer 10 minutes, stirring occasionally.

3. Add basil and parsley; purée with emersion blender or process in batches in container of blender. Return to heat and add cream and sour cream; simmer 1 minute.

4. Add Parmesan cheese, salt, and pepper, stirring until cheese melts. Garnish with croutons and shredded Parmesan cheese, if desired.

HAM & JARLSBERG SANDWICHES

Makes 6 sandwiches

¼ cup mayonnaise
2 tablespoons honey mustard
1 recipe Parmesan Rosemary Bread (recipe follows)
6 thin slices Virginia ham
6 thin slices Jarlsberg cheese

1. In small bowl, combine mayonnaise and honey mustard. Slice bread into ½-inch slices.

2. Using 2-inch square cutter, cut 12 squares of bread. Spread mayonnaise mixture evenly over one side of each bread slice. Top six slices with ham and cheese. Place remaining prepared bread over cheese.

PARMESAN ROSEMARY BREAD
Makes 1 loaf

2½ cups all-purpose flour
⅓ cup grated Parmesan cheese
1 tablespoon sugar
1 tablespoon chopped fresh rosemary
2 teaspoons dried minced onion
1 teaspoon baking soda
½ teaspoon salt
1 cup sour cream
⅓ cup milk
¼ cup butter, melted

1. Preheat oven to 350°.

2. Grease and flour 9x5x3-inch loaf pan.

3. In large bowl, combine flour, Parmesan cheese, sugar, rosemary, onion, baking soda, and salt. Add sour cream, milk, and butter.

4. Using electric mixer at medium speed, beat until ingredients are well combined.

5. Press dough in prepared loaf pan. Bake 35 to 40 minutes, or until wooden toothpick inserted in center comes out clean.

6. Cool in pan on wire rack 10 minutes. Remove from pan and cool completely on wire rack.

CREAMY HERBED SPINACH SOUP

GINGERBREAD FINGERS WITH ORANGE CRÈME FILLING

GINGERBREAD FINGERS WITH ORANGE CRÈME FILLING
Makes 10 fingers

1½ cups all-purpose flour
½ cup sugar
1 teaspoon baking soda
1 teaspoon ground ginger
½ teaspoon ground cinnamon
½ cup water
⅓ cup dark molasses
¼ cup butter, melted
1 large egg
½ teaspoon vanilla extract
1 recipe Orange Crème Filling (recipe follows)
Garnish: orange zest

1. Preheat oven to 350°.

2. Grease and flour 9-inch square pan. In medium bowl, combine flour, sugar, baking soda, ginger, and cinnamon.

3. In separate bowl, combine water, molasses, butter, egg, and vanilla extract, and using electric mixer at medium speed, beat until smooth.

4. Combine flour mixture and water mixture. Continue beating at medium speed, scraping down sides of bowl several times. Pour batter into prepared pan.

5. Bake 25 to 30 minutes, or until wooden toothpick inserted in center comes out clean. Cool in pan on wire rack 10 minutes. Remove from pan and let cool completely on wire rack.

6. With serrated knife, trim ¾-inch from each side of gingerbread; cut into approximately 4x1½-inch fingers.

7. Cut each finger in half horizontally and evenly spread orange crème filling on bottom half of gingerbread fingers; replace tops of gingerbread fingers. Garnish by piping additional orange crème on gingerbread and top with orange zest, if desired.

ROAST BEEF ROLL-UPS WITH MAYTAG BLUE CHEESE & CARAMELIZED ONIONS (Photo on page 116)
Makes 6 roll-ups

¾ cup Maytag blue cheese, crumbled
¼ cup mayonnaise
2 tablespoons sour cream
½ teaspoon freshly cracked black pepper
2 sun-dried tomato tortillas
2 spinach tortillas
½ pound thinly sliced roast beef
1 recipe Caramelized Onions (recipe follows)

1. In small bowl, combine blue cheese, mayonnaise, sour cream, and pepper.

2. Spread mixture evenly on tortillas, leaving ½-inch border. Evenly layer roast beef and caramelized onions on top of blue cheese mixture.

3. Roll up each tortilla, placing seam on bottom; trim ¼ inch off each end and slice in quarters.

CARAMELIZED ONIONS
Makes 1 cup

¼ cup butter
1½ pounds onions, sliced ⅛ inch thick
3 tablespoons Balsamic vinegar
½ teaspoon salt
¼ teaspoon ground black pepper

1. In large saucepan over medium-low heat, melt butter.

2. Add onions; cover and cook 30 minutes, stirring occasionally. Remove cover and increase heat to medium-high. Stir onions frequently until caramelized, about 20 minutes.

3. Add vinegar, salt, and pepper and stir until vinegar evaporates, 1 to 2 minutes.

ORANGE CRÈME FILLING
Makes 1 cup

1 (3-ounce) package cream cheese, softened
¼ cup butter, softened
1 teaspoon grated orange zest
1 cup confectioners' sugar

1. In medium bowl, combine cream cheese, butter, and orange zest; using electric mixer at medium speed, beat until smooth. Add confectioners' sugar and continue to beat until smooth.

DARK CHOCOLATE RASPBERRY MOUSSE CAKE
Makes 1 cake

2 cups all-purpose flour
2 teaspoons baking soda
½ teaspoon salt
2 cups sugar
½ cup butter, softened
½ cup buttermilk
⅓ cup dark cocoa powder
2 tablespoons vegetable oil
2 large eggs
1 teaspoon vanilla extract
1 cup boiling water
1 recipe Raspberry Mousse (recipe follows)
1 recipe Chocolate Ganache Icing (recipe follows)
Garnish: fresh raspberries, edible flowers

1. Preheat oven to 350°.

2. Grease and flour 3 (6x2-inch) cake pans. In medium bowl, combine flour, baking soda, and salt. In large bowl, combine sugar and butter.

3. Using electric mixer at medium speed, beat until creamy, scraping bowl often.

4. Add buttermilk, cocoa, oil, eggs, and vanilla extract; beat until smooth. Reduce speed to low and gradually add flour mixture, beating until moistened. Add boiling water, and beat at medium speed until smooth.

5. Pour batter into prepared pans. Bake 40 to 45 minutes, or until wooden toothpick inserted in center comes out clean; cool in pans on wire racks 10 minutes. Remove from pans and cool completely on wire racks.

6. To assemble, spread raspberry mousse on top of one cake layer and top with another cake layer; repeat. Pour chocolate ganache over center of cake, allowing excess to cover sides. Garnish with fresh raspberries and edible flowers, if desired.

RASPBERRY MOUSSE

2 tablespoons cold water
1 teaspoon unflavored gelatin
½ cup frozen raspberries, thawed
1 tablespoon lemon juice
½ cup sugar
1 tablespoon raspberry liqueur
½ cup heavy cream

1. In small microwave-safe ramekin, combine water and gelatin; let stand 5 minutes. Microwave 1 minute.

2. In container of blender, purée raspberries and lemon juice; strain to remove seeds.

3. In medium saucepan, combine raspberry purée and sugar over medium heat. Stir occasionally, until sugar dissolves, about 5 minutes. Stir in raspberry liqueur and dissolved gelatin.

4. Remove from heat and chill raspberry mixture 2 hours.

5. In medium bowl and using electric mixer at high speed, beat cream until stiff peaks form. Add raspberry mixture, beating 1 minute; chill 2 hours.

CHOCOLATE GANACHE ICING

1¼ cups heavy cream
¼ cup sugar
¼ cup corn syrup
1½ cups semisweet chocolate morsels

1. In medium saucepan over medium heat, combine cream, sugar, and corn syrup, stirring until sugar dissolves. Stir in chocolate until melted. Cool slightly before use.

festive
COOKBOOK

Seasonal Scones

WHETHER A FRUITY INGREDIENT OR GINGER ENHANCED, THE RICH FLAVORS OF THESE DESSERTS COMPLEMENT A WARM CUP OF TEA. SIDE DOLLOPS OF WHIPPED CREAM WITH A SPRINKLE OF CINNAMON OR ORANGE ZEST ADD THE FINAL TOUCH.

ORANGE FIG SCONES

✤ Warm scones are a must during the holidays. A touch of cream or favorite fruit preserves add to the rich fig flavor of our Orange Fig Scones. The Gingerbread Scones, at right, have more of a peppery ginger flavor enhanced with holiday spices of cinnamon and cloves. Here we have cut scones out of the dough to make a fun gingerbread man shape instead of a traditional triangle shape. These pair well with a gingerbread house or other holiday decorations you may have in your home. Once their baked brushed egg glazes brown nicely, both will shine as stars of your holiday desserts.

GINGERBREAD SCONES

ORANGE FIG SCONES
Makes 12 scones

- 2 cups all-purpose flour
- ¼ cup plus 2 tablespoons sugar, divided
- 1½ teaspoons baking powder
- ½ teaspoon salt
- 6 tablespoons butter
- ⅔ cup chopped dried figs
- 2 tablespoons orange zest
- 2 large eggs, divided
- ½ cup heavy cream
- 1 teaspoon vanilla extract

1. Preheat oven to 400°. Line 2 baking sheets with parchment paper.

2. In a large bowl, combine flour, ¼ cup sugar, baking powder, and salt. Using pastry blender, cut in butter until a mixture is crumbly. Add figs and orange zest; mix well.

3. In a separate bowl, whisk together 1 egg, heavy cream, and vanilla extract. Add to flour mixture, and stir until dough is just combined; dough will be sticky.

4. Divide dough into two balls. On a lightly floured surface, roll half of dough into a 6x½-inch circle; cut into 6 wedges. Repeat process for remaining dough.

5. In a small bowl, lightly beat remaining egg. Brush scones with beaten egg and sprinkle with remaining sugar. Place on prepared baking sheets; bake for 12 to 14 minutes, or until lightly browned.

GINGERBREAD SCONES
Makes 12 scones

- 2 cups self-rising flour
- ¼ cup firmly packed dark brown sugar
- 1½ teaspoons ground ginger
- 1 teaspoon ground cinnamon
- ⅛ teaspoon ground cloves
- ½ cup cold unsalted butter, cut into cubes
- ⅓ cup buttermilk
- ⅓ cup unsulfured molasses
- 1 large egg, lightly beaten
- 2 pieces candied ginger, cut into ⅛-inch squares
- 1 cup cold heavy cream
- 3 tablespoons confectioners' sugar

1. Preheat oven to 400°. Line a baking sheet with parchment paper; set aside.

2. In a large bowl, whisk together the flour, brown sugar, ginger, cinnamon, and cloves. Using a pastry blender, cut butter into flour mixture until mixture resembles coarse meal.

3. In a medium bowl, whisk together the buttermilk and molasses. Add buttermilk mixture to flour mixture, and stir until dough is just combined (dough will be sticky).

4. Transfer dough to a lightly floured surface, and pat into a ½-inch-thick circle; using a small gingerbread-man cutter, cut 12 scones, gathering scraps and rerolling as necessary.

5. Place scones on the prepared baking sheet. Using a pastry brush, brush tops of scones with beaten egg, and place two squares of candied ginger on center of body to make buttons. Bake for 8 minutes, or until golden brown. Transfer to a wire rack to cool.

6. In a large bowl and using an electric mixer at medium-high speed, beat the cream and confectioners' sugar until soft peaks form. Serve scones with whipped cream.

festive
COOKBOOK

MENU
*Creamy Cranberry-White
 Chocolate Delight*
Spirited Eggnog Coffee Punch
Orange Hot Chocolate
Chai Latte
Candy Cane Cocoa Coffee
Butter Rum Cider

Warm-the-Heart Pleasures

A CALMING PRELUDE TO A CHILLY WINTER DAY OR AN ESPECIALLY SWEET START TO A MEMORABLE CHRISTMAS MORNING, THESE HOT DRINKS WILL WARM YOU TO YOUR TOES.

SPIRITED EGGNOG
COFFEE PUNCH
(RECIPE ON PG. 124)

CREAMY CRANBERRY-WHITE CHOCOLATE DELIGHT

Makes 6 to 8 servings

- 3 (4-ounce) bars white chocolate, chopped
- 2 cups heavy whipping cream, divided
- 3 cups whole milk
- 3 cups cranberry juice
- Fresh cranberries (optional)
- White chocolate curls (optional)

1. In a large saucepan over medium heat, add chocolate; gradually whisk in 1½ cups cream, whisking constantly until chocolate is melted. Whisk in milk and cranberry juice; cook until heated through. Whisk in remaining ½ cup cream. Garnish with skewered cranberries, and top with white chocolate curls, if desired.

ORANGE HOT CHOCOLATE

CHAI LATTE

SPIRITED EGGNOG COFFEE PUNCH
(Photo on page 122)
Makes 6 to 8 servings

4 cups eggnog
3 cups hot strong coffee
1 cup bourbon
3 tablespoons cinnamon syrup*
Whipped cream (optional)
Ground cinnamon (optional)

1. In a large saucepan, heat eggnog and coffee over medium heat until hot. Stir in bourbon and cinnamon syrup. Top each serving with whipped cream, and sprinkle with cinnamon, if desired. Serve immediately.

*For testing purposes, our test kitchen used Monin Cinnamon Premium Gourmet Syrup. Available at *monin.com*.

ORANGE HOT CHOCOLATE
Makes 6 to 8 servings

½ cup sugar
1 cup unsweetened cocoa powder
4 cups heavy whipping cream
4 cups whole milk
8 ounces dark chocolate, chopped
1 cup orange-flavored liqueur
Sugared orange slices (optional)

1. In a large saucepan, heat sugar and cocoa over medium heat. Gradually whisk in cream and milk until smooth. Cook, whisking constantly, until tiny bubbles form around the edge of the pan. Add chocolate, stirring until melted. Remove from heat; stir in liqueur. Serve each with a sugared orange slice, if desired.

vintage sparkle
Beautiful aged notes are reminiscent of those we have received in the past. Simple and quaint, they are especially nice handwritten from the heart. Available from Touch of Europe, *www.touchofeurope.net*.

CHAI LATTE
Makes 12 to 14 servings

8 cups water
4 cups whole milk
¾ cup sugar
3 orange slices
2 cinnamon sticks
1 tablespoon whole cloves
1 whole nutmeg, grated
¾ teaspoon whole black peppercorns
6 black tea bags
Cinnamon sticks (optional)

1. In a large Dutch oven, combine water, milk, sugar, orange slices, cinnamon sticks, cloves, nutmeg, peppercorns, and tea bags. Bring to a boil over medium-high heat, and cook, stirring until sugar dissolves. Remove from heat; let stand 15 minutes. Garnish with cinnamon sticks, if desired.

CANDY CANE COCOA COFFEE
Makes 12 to 14 servings

1½ cups unsweetened cocoa powder
1½ cups sugar
6 cups hot strong coffee
9 cups whole milk
1½ teaspoons peppermint extract
Peppermint sticks (optional)

1. In a large Dutch oven, combine cocoa and sugar. Gradually whisk in coffee and milk, and heat over medium-high heat until tiny bubbles form around the edge of the pan. Remove from heat; stir in extract. Garnish with peppermint sticks, if desired.

BUTTER RUM CIDER
Makes 12 to 14 servings

12 cups apple cider
3 tablespoons chopped fresh ginger
1½ teaspoons whole allspice
1½ teaspoons whole cloves
1 whole nutmeg, grated
2 cinnamon sticks
1½ cups butterscotch schnapps liqueur
Apple slices (optional)

1. In a large Dutch oven, add cider, ginger, allspice, cloves, nutmeg, and cinnamon sticks; bring to a boil over medium-high heat. Remove from heat; stir in liqueur. Let stand 10 minutes. Strain, discarding solids, and serve. Top with apples slices, if desired.

Recipe Index

Appetizers
Asparagus-Prosciutto Puffs 109
Cherry Tomatoes with Jalapeño-Pimiento Cheese 109
Ham & Jarlsberg Sandwiches 117
Mini Potato Skins with Horseradish Dipping Sauce 112
Pizza Rolls with Marinara Sauce 112
Prosciutto and Brie Dip 112
Roasted Beef Finger Sandwiches with Kalamata Mustard Butter 105
Roast Beef Roll-Ups with Maytag Blue Cheese & Caramelized Onions 118
Shrimp Mousse wth Saffron Aïoli in Phyllo Cups 105

Beverages
Butter Rum Cider 125
Candy Cane Cocoa Coffee 125
Chai Latte 125
Cranberry Splash 99
Creamy Cranberry-White Chocolate Delight 123
Holiday Tea 88
Hot Rum Punch 115
Orange Hot Chocolate 124
Ruby Sangria 109
Sparkling Brunch Punch 95
Spirited Eggnog Coffee Punch 124

Bread
Cranberry Muffins with Orange Crumble Topping 95
Easy Orange Rolls 101
Gingerbread Scones 121
Honey Scones with Apricot Preserves 106
Orange Fig Scones 121
Parmesan Rosemary Bread 117
Sweet Potato Pecan Muffins 99

Desserts
Amaretto Cheesecake Squares 114
Biscotti Christmas Tree 76
Brandy Cream in Chocolate Cups 106
Dark Chocolate Raspberry Mousse Cake 119
Double Fudge Brownie Pops 74
Gingerbread Fingers with Orange Crème Filling 118
Hello Dolly Bar Cookies 84
Kahlúa and Coffee Fudge 114
Karen's Cocoons 84
Lemon Glazed Miniature Cakes 107
Meringue Surprises 84
Oatmeal Cookies 85
Pecan Pie Tartlets 113
Spiced Chocolate Truffles 88
Spiced Jam Tartlets 88
White-Chocolate Mousse Cake 103

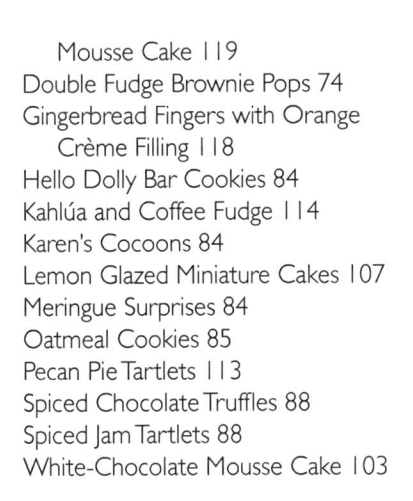

Icings, Glaze, Filling, and Toppings
Chocolate Ganache Icing 119
Granola Nut Topping 96
Marmalade Icing 76
Orange Crème Filling 119
Orange Crumble Topping 95
Orange Glaze 101
Raspberry Mousse 119
Strawberry Sauce 103

Main Dishes
Deep-Fried Turkey 102
Ham, Mushroom, and Spinach Strata 96
Sausage Breakfast Casserole 99

Miscellaneous
Caramelized Onions 118
Cinnamon-Spiced Crabapples 73
Creamy Balsamic Italian Dressing 101
Horseradish Dipping Sauce 112
Jalapeño-Pimiento Cheese 109
Marinara Sauce 113
Saffron Aïoli 105
Sugared Almonds 106

Preserves
Apricot Preserves 106

Salad
Holiday Italian Salad 101

Sides
Broccoli & Cheese Stuffed Potatoes 102
Cornbread Dressing 103
Double Cheese Grits Casserole 99
Glazed Carrots 103
Herbed Home Fries with Caramelized Onions 95
Hot Baked Fruit with Granola Nut Topping 96
Hot Curried Fruit 99
Squash and Zucchini Casserole 101

Soup
Creamy Herbed Spinach Soup 117

Reader Resources
Cover tree from Joaquin Hernandez of J&H Christmas Trees LLC, 205-281-2036 or 336-325-0811

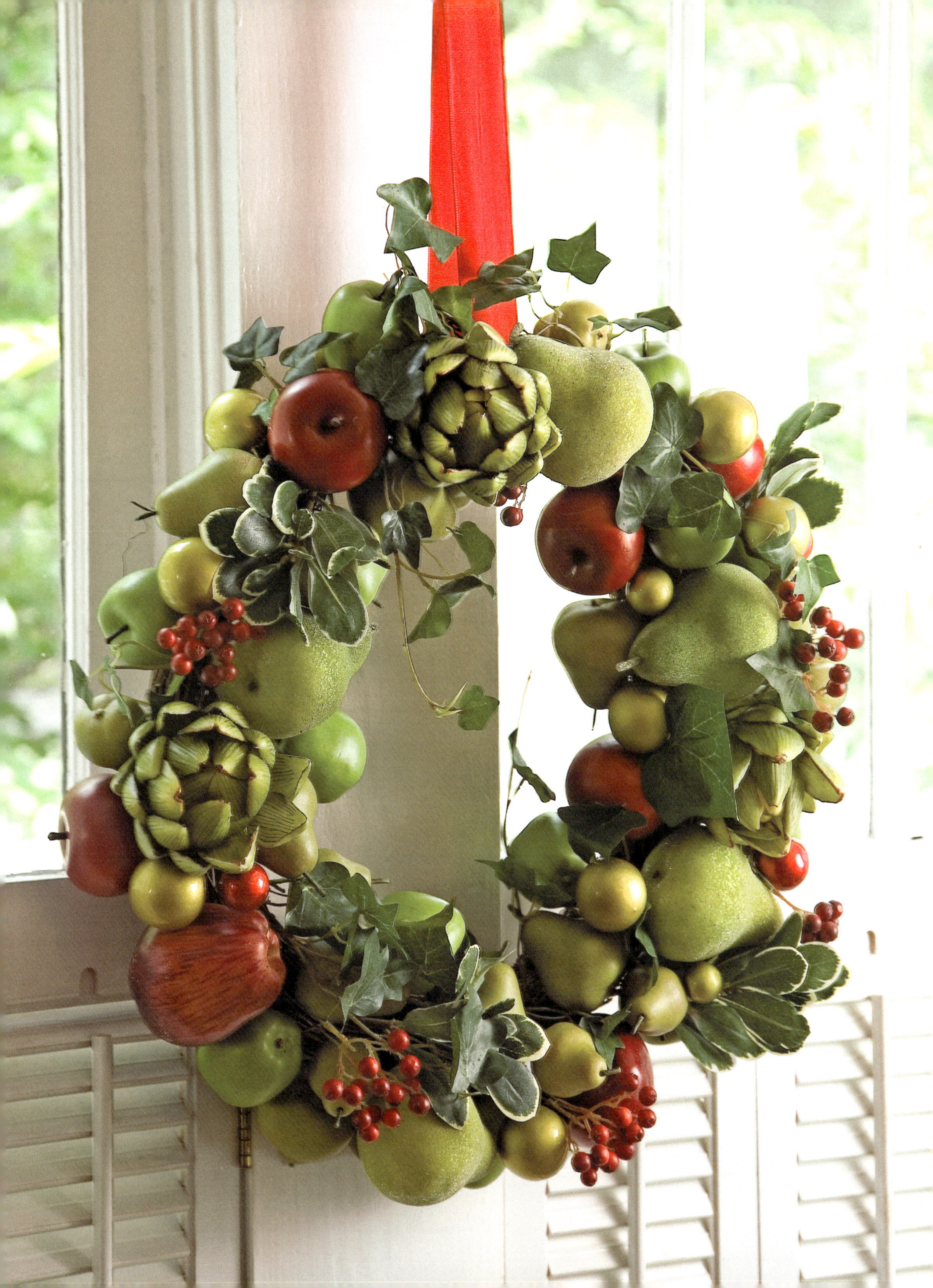

craft it
QUICKLY

closing craft
Long strips of wide ribbon display holiday greetings from friends. Staple the inside of the card to the ribbon so all can enjoy the greeting.

128 | CHRISTMAS cottage

CPSIA information can be obtained
at www.ICGtesting.com
Printed in the USA
LVIC06n1740181113
361784LV00051B/729